WITHDRAWN
UTSA LIBRARIES

Zeuthen Lecture Book Series
Karl Gunnar Persson, editor

Modeling Bounded Rationality
Ariel Rubinstein

Forecasting Non-stationary Economic Time Series
Michael P. Clements and David E. Hendry

Political Economics: Explaining Economic Policy
Torsten Persson and Guido Tabellini

Wage Dispersion: Why are Similar Workers Paid Differently?
Dale T. Mortensen

Competition and Growth: Reconciling Theory and Evidence
Philippe Aghion and Rachel Griffith

Product Variety and the Gains from International Trade
Robert C. Feenstra

*Unemployment Fluctuations and Stabilization Policies:
A New Keynesian Perspective*
Jordi Galí

Unemployment Fluctuations and Stabilization Policies

Unemployment Fluctuations and Stabilization Policies

A New Keynesian Perspective

Jordi Galí

The MIT Press
Cambridge, Massachusetts
London, England

© 2011 Massachusetts Institute of Technology

All rights reserved. No part of this book may be reproduced in any form by any electronic or mechanical means (including photocopying, recording, or information storage and retrieval) without permission in writing from the publisher.

For information about special quantity discounts, please email special_sales@mitpress.mit.edu

This book was set in Palatino by Aptara Inc. Printed and bound in the United States of America.

Library of Congress Cataloging-in-Publication Data

Galí, Jordi, 1961–
Unemployment fluctuations and stabilization policies : a new keynesian perspective / Jordi Galí.
  p. cm. – (Zeuthen lectures)
Includes bibliographical references and index.
ISBN 978-0-262-01597-4 (hardcover : alk. paper)   1. Unemployment.
2. Unemployment – Government policy.   3. Monetary policy.
4. Keynesian economics.   I. Title.

HD5707.5.G36 2011
339.5'3 – dc22   2010047659

10 9 8 7 6 5 4 3 2 1

For Ellen

Contents

	Series Foreword	ix
	Preface	xi
	Introduction	**1**
1	**A Simple Model of Unemployment and Inflation Dynamics**	**7**
2	**Unemployment, the Output Gap, and the Welfare Costs of Economic Fluctuations**	**37**
3	**Unemployment and Monetary Policy Design in the New Keynesian Model**	**61**
4	**Concluding Remarks and Directions for Future Research**	**83**
	Appendix A	**89**
	Appendix B	**91**
	Appendix C	**93**
	Appendix D	**95**
	References	97
	Index	103

Series Foreword

The Zeuthen Lectures offer a forum for leading scholars to develop and synthesize novel results in theoretical and applied economics. The Zeuthen Lectures are organized by the Institute of Economics, University of Copenhagen. The aim is to present advances in knowledge in a form accessible to a wide audience of economists and advanced students of economics. The topics range from abstract theorizing to economic history. Regardless of the choice of topic, the emphasis in the lecture series is on originality and relevance.
The lecture series is named after Frederik Zeuthen, a former professor at the Institute of Economics.

Karl Gunnar Persson

Preface

Presented in this book is a revised version of the Zeuthen Lectures I delivered at the University of Copenhagen on March 17 to 19, 2010. In these lectures I develop a version of the standard New Keynesian model for which a concept of unemployment can be defined, and show how it can account reasonably well for the observed properties of unemployment fluctuations. I use the same framework also to construct unemployment-based measures of the output gap, which are compared with more conventional measures. Last, I study the gains from having the central bank respond systematically to the unemployment rate, in addition to other variables.

I am thankful to Karl Gunnar Persson, Christian Schultz, Henrik Jensen, and others of the Department of Economics at the University of Copenhagen for their comments and hospitality during my visit. I have also benefited from comments by seminar participants at the Riksbank, Federal Reserve Board, CREI-UPF, ECB, and NBER Summer Institute. Tomaz Cajner, Alain Schlaepfer, and Lien Laureys provided excellent research assistance. The research leading to this volume has received funding from the European Research Council under the European Union's Seventh Framework Programme (FP7/2007-2013)/ ERC grant agreement 229650.

Introduction

For the past fifteen years the New Keynesian model has served as a frame of reference for analyses of fluctuations and stabilization policies.[1] That framework has allowed the rigor and internal consistency of dynamic general equilibrium models to be combined with typically Keynesian assumptions, like monopolistic competition and nominal rigidities, thus setting the stage for a meaningful, welfare-based analysis of the effects of alternative monetary policy rules. Indeed many central banks and policy institutions have adopted medium-scale versions of that model for simulation and forecasting purposes.[2]

---

1. For a textbook exposition of the New Keynesian model, see Walsh (2003), Woodford (2003), Galí (2008), and Walsh (2010). An early version and analysis of the baseline New Keynesian model can be found in Yun (1996), who used a discrete-time version of the staggered price-setting model originally developed in Calvo (1983). King and Wolman (1996) provided a detailed analysis of the steady state and dynamic properties of the model. Goodfriend and King (1997), Rotemberg and Woodford (1999a), and Clarida, Galí, and Gertler (1999) were among the first to conduct a normative policy analysis using that framework.

2. See, for example Smets and Wouters (2003, 2007) and Christiano, Eichenbaum, and Evans (2005). For a descriptions of versions of those models developed at policy institutions, see Christoffel, Coenen, and Warne (2008),

But success breeds criticism, and the New Keynesian model has been no exception. Among other shortcomings the lack of reference to unemployment is often pointed to as one of the model's main weaknesses. This is not surprising given the central role of that variable in the policy debate and in public perceptions of the costs associated with business cycles. Furthermore the conspicuous absence of unemployment from the standard New Keynesian model could even be interpreted as suggesting that central banks need not monitor or respond to unemployment in a systematic way. It may seem that through the lens of the New Keynesian model, unemployment and the frictions underlying it are not essential for understanding fluctuations in nominal and real variables, nor a key ingredient in the design of monetary policy.

Yet, over the past few years, a growing number of researchers have sought to rectify that anomaly by developing frameworks that combine the nominal rigidities and consequent monetary nonneutralities of the New Keynesian model with labor market imperfections that give rise to unemployment. Those frictions are generally introduced by embedding a labor market with search and matching, in the tradition of Mortensen and Pissarides (1994), into some version of the New Keynesian model.[3] The resulting framework has been used in both positive and normative applications, with and without the assumption of wage rigidities.[4]

In the present book I propose a different approach to introducing unemployment in the New Keynesian framework.

Edge, Kiley, and Laforte (2007), and Erceg, Guerrieri, and Gust (2006), among others.

3. See Alexopoulos (2006) for an alternative approach, based on an efficiency wage model of the labor market, albeit in the context of a monetary model with no (exogenous) nominal rigidities.

4. Walsh (2003, 2005) and Trigari (2009) analyzed the impact of embedding labor market frictions into the basic New Keynesian model with sticky

My approach, based on Galí (2011a), involves a *reinterpretation* of the labor market in the standard New Keynesian model with staggered wage setting, as originally formulated by Erceg, Henderson, and Levin (2000), rather than a modification or an extension of that model. The resulting framework preserves the convenience of the representative household paradigm, and allows one to determine the equilibrium levels of employment, the labor force, and hence the unemployment rate (as well as other macro variables of interest) conditional on the monetary policy rule in place. Unemployment in the model results from the presence of market power in labor markets, reflected in a positive average wage markup, namely a positive gap between the prevailing wage and the disutility of work (expressed in terms of consumption) for the marginal worker employed. On the other hand, fluctuations in the unemployment rate are associated with variations in that average wage markup due to the presence of nominal wage rigidities.[5]

---

prices but flexible wages, with a focus on the size and persistence of the effects of monetary policy shocks.

More recent contributions have extended that work in two dimensions. First, they have relaxed the assumption of flexible wages, and introduced different forms of nominal and real wage rigidity. The work of Trigari (2006) and Christoffel and Linzert (2005) falls into that category. Second, the focus of analysis has gradually turned to normative issues, and more specifically, to the implications of labor market frictions and unemployment for the design of monetary policy. See, for example, the work of Blanchard and Galí (2010) in a model with real wage rigidities, Faia (2009, 2010), and Thomas (2008).

More recently Christiano, Trabandt, and Walentin (2010) have modified the new Keynesian model by embedding in it an alternative model of unemployment, where the probability of finding a job is increasing in search effort, and where imperfect risk sharing among individuals is a consequence of the unobservability of effort.

5. The general approach builds on Galí (1996). Recent applications of that approach to the New Keynesian model can be found in Blanchard and Galí (2007), Galí (2011a), and, closely related to the latter (but developed independently), Casares (2010).

An important advantage of the proposed approach lies in its compatibility with a variety of assumptions regarding aspects of the model unrelated to unemployment, including the specific forms of price and wage rigidities, household utility, or the determinants of variable desired markups. Still the proposed framework has limitations. In particular, it abstracts from potential sources of unemployment other than noncompetitive wages, including those associated with the costly reallocation of labor across firms or sectors (in terms of time and other resources) that can give rise to frictional unemployment. It is important to recognize, however, that the findings of the recent literature on labor market frictions suggest that frictional unemployment is not enough to generate unemployment fluctuations of the size and persistence observed in the data, and that suggest need for some kind of wage rigidity.[6]

The content of the book following the present introduction is organized as follows. In chapter 1, I develop the basic model of unemployment that is used throughout the book, embedding it in a standard New Keynesian framework with staggered price and wage setting, similar to that in Erceg, Henderson, and Levin (2000). Using a calibrated version of the latter, I analyze its implied predictions regarding the properties of unemployment in response to shocks of diverse nature, when the central bank follows a conventional Taylor rule. The analysis puts special emphasis on the role played by nominal wage rigidities in accounting for the volatility and persistence of unemployment. A conclusion of that quantitative exercise is that realistic wage rigidities may potentially generate fluctuations in unemployment with cyclical properties not much different from those observed in the US and euro area economies.

---

6. See, for example, Hall (2005), Gertler and Trigari (2009), Galí (2011b), and Shimer (2005, 2010).

In chapter 2, I explore the relationship between economic fluctuations and efficiency using the New Keynesian framework developed in the first chapter. In particular, I develop a measure of the *output gap*, namely the deviation between the efficient and the actual levels of output. Under some assumptions, the output gap is shown to be a function of the price and wage markups, which can be expressed in turn in terms of two observable variables: the labor income share and the unemployment rate. For the United States the resulting output gap turns out to be positively correlated with "traditional" measures of economic slack, like the Hodrick–Prescott detrended GDP, though this is not so much the case for the euro area. In addition I consider the implications for welfare of the output gap and its fluctuations, by computing a measure of the associated utility losses and analyzing its changes over time. The findings of that exercise point to small average welfare losses resulting from output gap fluctuations, despite the substantial variations in the size of those losses over the cycle; still the losses experienced in recession episodes are far from negligible.

In chapter 3, I turn to the relation between unemployment and the design of monetary policy. This discussion is partly motivated by the tight link, both theoretical and empirical, between the output gap and the unemployment rate as shown in the previous chapter. That link, together with the near-optimality of output gap stabilization in an environment with stickiness in both prices and wages (as uncovered by the literature), points to the desirability of policies that put some weight on unemployment stabilization. Thus I begin with an analysis of unemployment and several other macro variables under the optimal monetary policy and compare it to that prevailing under a standard Taylor rule. That analysis suggests the presence of likely welfare gains from stabilizing the unemployment rate beyond what is implied by the Taylor rule. This is confirmed by the study of the properties of a more general interest rate rule, one that allows for a systematic response to unemployment and wage inflation, in addition to output and price inflation. In particular, I show how a simple rule that responds to price inflation and the unemployment rate can approximate reasonably well the optimal policy rule. Perhaps more surprisingly, the same simple rule is shown to account quite accurately for the observed patterns in the federal funds rate during the Greenspan era, at least until the deflation scare of 2003.

Finally, in chapter 4, I offer some tentative conclusions, review some of the shortcomings of the proposed approach, and point to possible directions for future research.

1 A Simple Model of Unemployment and Inflation Dynamics

The New Keynesian model with staggered wage and price setting of Erceg, Henderson, and Levin (2000; henceforth, EHL) constitutes the core of the dynamic stochastic general equilibrium (DSGE) frameworks that have become popular in recent years, and that have been adopted by many central banks and policy institutions as an analytical tool. While the EHL model lacks many of the bells and whistles that have been incorporated in the estimated medium-scale models, it remains useful in elucidating the implications of nominal rigidities for the design of monetary policy.[1]

The variant presented here, based on Galí (2011a), treats labor as being indivisible in that each period a given individual works a fixed number of hours or does not work at all. As a result all variations in labor input take place at the extensive margin (i.e., in the form of variations in employment). Since that margin dominates the observed variations in total hours of work, the assumption of indivisible labor remains a good first approximation. Most important,

---

1. See Christiano, Eichenbaum, and Evans (2005) and Smets and Wouters (2003, 2007) for examples of estimated medium-scale models built on the EHL model.

however, that assumption leads to a definition of unemployment that is consistent with its empirical counterpart.

In the second half of the chapter, I analyze the equilibrium properties of unemployment in response to a variety of shocks, using a calibrated version of the New Keynesian model. I keep the focus on the relation between the degree of nominal wage rigidities and the model's implied volatility and persistence of unemployment.

Next I describe the components of a variant of the EHL model. The model's equilibrium is described by the same set of equations as in EHL, to which I add an equation describing the evolution of unemployment. The reader is referred to the original EHL paper for the details on some of the derivations.[2]

1.1 Households, Wage Setting, and Unemployment

The economy is assumed to have a large number of identical households. Each household has a continuum of members represented by the unit square and indexed by a pair $(i, j) \in [0, 1] \times [0, 1]$. The first index, $i \in [0, 1]$, represents the type of labor service in which a given household member is specialized. The second index, $j \in [0, 1]$, determines the disutility from work. The latter is given by $\chi_t j^\varphi$ if he is employed and zero otherwise, where $\varphi \geq 0$ and $\chi_t > 0$ is an exogenous preference shifter (often referred to below as a labor supply shock). Utility from consumption is separable and logarithmic in a CES index of the quantities consumed of the different goods available. As in Merz (1995) and much of

---

2. See also Galí (2008, ch. 6) for a version of the EHL model consistent with the notation used here.

A Simple Model of Unemployment and Inflation Dynamics

the subsequent literature, I assume full risk sharing within the household. Given the separability of preferences, this implies the same level of consumption for all household members, independently of their work status. This is not an innocuous assumption, especially from a welfare standpoint, but one that I stick to in order to preserve the model's tractability.[3]

The household's period utility is given by the integral of its members' period utilities and can thus be written as

$$U(C_t, \{N_t(i)\}; \chi_t) \equiv \log C_t - \chi_t \int_0^1 \int_0^{N_t(i)} j^\varphi \, dj \, di$$

$$= \log C_t - \chi_t \int_0^1 \frac{N_t(i)^{1+\varphi}}{1+\varphi} di,$$

where $C_t \equiv \left(\int_0^1 C_t(z)^{1-(1/\epsilon_p)} dz \right)^{\epsilon_p/(\epsilon_p - 1)}$, $C_t(z)$ is the quantity consumed of good z, for $i \in [0, 1]$, and $N_t(i) \in [0, 1]$ is the fraction of members specialized in type i labor who are employed in period t. Below I assume that $\xi_t \equiv \log \chi_t$ follows the AR(1) process:

$$\xi_t = \rho_\xi \xi_{t-1} + \varepsilon_t^\xi,$$

where $\rho_\xi \in [0, 1]$ and ε_t^ξ is a white noise process with zero mean and variance σ_ξ^2.

Each household is assumed to maximize

$$E_0 \sum_{t=0}^\infty \beta^t U(C_t, \{N_t(i)\}; \chi_t)$$

---

[3]. See Christiano, Trabandt, and Walentin (2010) for an unemployment model with separable preferences but different levels of consumption for employed and not-employed household members.

subject to a sequence of flow budget constraints given by

$$\int_0^1 P_t(z)C_t(z)dz + Q_t B_t \leq B_{t-1}$$
$$+ \int_0^1 W_t(i)N_t(i)di + \Pi_t, \quad (1.1)$$

where $P_t(z)$ is the price of good z, $W_t(i)$ is the nominal wage for type i labor, B_t represents purchases of a nominally riskless one-period discount bond paying one monetary unit, Q_t is the price of that bond, and Π_t is a lump-sum component of income (which may include, among other items, dividends from the ownership of firms). The sequence above of period budget constraints is supplemented with a solvency condition which prevents the household from engaging in Ponzi schemes.

Optimal demand for each good resulting from utility maximization takes the familiar form:

$$C_t(z) = \left(\frac{P_t(z)}{P_t}\right)^{-\epsilon_p} C_t, \quad (1.2)$$

where $P_t \equiv \left(\int_0^1 P_t(z)^{1-\epsilon_p} dz\right)^{1/1-\epsilon_p}$ denotes the price index for final goods. Note also that (1.2) implies that total consumption expenditures can be written as $\int_0^1 P_t(z)C_t(z)dz = P_t C_t$.

The household's intertemporal optimality condition is given by

$$Q_t = \beta E_t \left\{ \frac{C_t}{C_{t+1}} \frac{P_t}{P_{t+1}} \right\}. \quad (1.3)$$

As discussed below, I assume that the wage for each labor type $W_t(i)$ is set by the workers specialized in that type of labor (or a union representing them), whereas the corresponding employment level $N_t(i)$ is determined by the aggregation of firms' labor demand decisions (and allocated uniformly across households). Thus both $W_t(i)$ and $N_t(i)$ are taken as given by each individual household.

More specifically, and following Calvo's formalism (Calvo 1983), I assume that workers specialized in a given type of labor (or the union representing them) reset their *nominal* wage with probability $1 - \theta_w$ each period. That probability is independent of the time elapsed since those workers last reset their wage, in addition to being independent across labor types. Thus a fraction θ_w keep their wage unchanged in any given period, making that parameter a natural index of nominal wage rigidities.

When reoptimizing their wage in period t, workers choose a wage W_t^* in order to maximize their households' utility (as opposed to their individual utility), taking as given all aggregate variables, including the aggregate wage index $W_t \equiv \left(\int_0^1 W_t(i)^{1-\epsilon_w} di\right)^{1/(1-\epsilon_w)}$. That maximization problem is subject to a sequence of flow budget constraints as in (1.1), as well as a sequence of labor demand schedules of the form

$$N_{t+k|t} = \left(\frac{W_t^*}{W_{t+k}}\right)^{-\epsilon_w} \int_0^1 N_{t+k}(z) dz, \tag{1.4}$$

where $N_{t+k|t}$ denotes the quantity demanded in period $t + k$ of a labor type whose wage was last reset in period t and $N_{t+k}(z)$ is firm z's employment index defined below. Note that (1.4) can be derived from cost minimization by firms, as discussed below.

The first-order condition associated with the wage-setting problem can be written as

$$\sum_{k=0}^{\infty} (\beta \theta_w)^k E_t \left\{ \frac{N_{t+k|t}}{C_{t+k}} \left(\frac{W_t^*}{P_{t+k}} - \mathcal{M}^w MRS_{t+k|t} \right) \right\} = 0,$$

where $MRS_{t+k|t} \equiv \chi_t C_t N_{t+k|t}^{\varphi}$ is the period $t+k$ marginal rate of substitution between consumption and employment for a worker whose wage is reset in period t, and $\mathcal{M}^w \equiv \epsilon_w/(\epsilon_w - 1)$, is the desired or frictionless wage markup, namely the constant ratio between the real wage and the marginal rate of substitution that would obtain under flexible wages (corresponding to $\theta_w = 0$).

Log-linearizing the optimality condition above around the perfect foresight zero inflation steady state, and using lower case letters to denote the logs of the original variables, we obtain the approximate wage-setting rule

$$w_t^* = \mu^w + (1 - \beta\theta_w) \sum_{k=0}^{\infty} (\beta\theta_w)^k E_t \{mrs_{t+k|t} + p_{t+k}\}, \quad (1.5)$$

where $\mu^w \equiv \log \mathcal{M}_w$. Note that in the absence of nominal wage rigidities ($\theta_w = 0$), we have $w_t^* = w_t = \mu^w + mrs_t + p_t$, implying a constant (log) markup μ^w of the wage w_t over the price-adjusted marginal rate of substitution, $mrs_t + p_t$. When nominal wage rigidities are present, new wages are set instead as a constant markup μ^w over a weighted average of current and expected future price-adjusted marginal rates of substitution.

I define the economy's *average* marginal rate of substitution as $MRS_t \equiv \chi_t C_t N_t^{\varphi}$, where $N_t \equiv \int_0^1 N_t(i) di$ is the aggregate employment rate. Thus we can write (after taking logs)

$$mrs_{t+k|t} = mrs_{t+k} + \varphi(n_{t+k|t} - n_{t+k}) \quad (1.6)$$
$$= mrs_{t+k} - \epsilon_w \varphi(w_t^* - w_{t+k}).$$

Furthermore, log-linearizing the expression for the aggregate wage index around a zero inflation steady state, we obtain

$$w_t = \theta_w w_{t-1} + (1 - \theta_w) w_t^*. \quad (1.7)$$

A Simple Model of Unemployment and Inflation Dynamics 13

We finally combine equations (1.5) through (1.7) and derive the baseline wage inflation equation

$$\pi_t^w = \beta E_t\{\pi_{t+1}^w\} - \lambda_w(\mu_t^w - \mu^w), \tag{1.8}$$

where $\pi_t^w \equiv w_t - w_{t-1}$ is wage inflation, $\mu_t^w \equiv w_t - p_t - mrs_t$ denotes the (log) *average* wage markup, and $\lambda_w \equiv [(1 - \theta_w)(1 - \beta\theta_w)]/[\theta_w(1 + \epsilon_w\varphi)] > 0$. In words, wage inflation depends positively on expected one-period-ahead wage inflation and negatively on the deviation of the average wage markup from its desired value. The wage inflation equation (1.8) is a key condition in standard representations of the equilibrium dynamics of the New Keynesian model in the presence of monopolistic competition and staggered wage setting in the labor market.

Next, and following my previous work (Galí 2011a), I show how unemployment can be introduced in the framework, allowing the wage inflation equation (1.8) to be reformulated in terms of the unemployment rate.

1.1.1 Introducing Unemployment

Consider an individual specialized in type i labor and with disutility of work $\chi_t j^\varphi$. Using household welfare as a criterion, and *taking as given current labor market conditions* (as summarized by the wage prevailing in his trade) that individual will be willing to work in period t if and only if

$$\frac{W_t(i)}{P_t} \geq \chi_t C_t j^\varphi,$$

namely if and only if the real wage for his labor type exceeds his disutility of labor, where the latter is expressed in terms of consumption using the household's marginal valuation of income.

Thus the marginal supplier of type i labor, which I denote by $L_t(i)$, is given by

$$\frac{W_t(i)}{P_t} = \chi_t C_t L_t(i)^\varphi. \tag{1.9}$$

I define the aggregate labor force (or participation rate) as $L_t \equiv \int_0^1 L_t(i)di$. So, after taking logs and integrating over i, the following approximate relation can be derived:

$$w_t - p_t = c_t + \varphi l_t + \xi_t \tag{1.10}$$

where $\xi_t \equiv \log \chi_t$, and where I have made use of the first-order approximations $w_t \simeq \int_0^1 w_t(i)di$ and $l_t \simeq \int_0^1 l_t(i)di$ around the symmetric steady state. Equation (1.10) can be thought of as an aggregate labor supply or participation condition.

Following Galí (2010), I define the unemployment rate u_t as the log difference between the labor force and employment:

$$u_t \equiv l_t - n_t. \tag{1.11}$$

This definition of the unemployment rate is, for practical purposes and given the low observed unemployment rates, very close to the conventional one, namely $1 - (N_t/L_t)$.[4]

The definition of the average wage markup $\mu_t^w \equiv (w_t - p_t) - (c_t + \varphi n_t + \xi_t)$ combined with (1.10) and (1.11) one can obtain the following simple linear relation between the wage markup and the unemployment rate:

$$\mu_t^w = \varphi u_t. \tag{1.12}$$

---

4. Note that $1 - (N_t/L_t) = 1 - \exp\{-u_t\} \simeq u_t$ for unemployment rates near zero.

A Simple Model of Unemployment and Inflation Dynamics 15

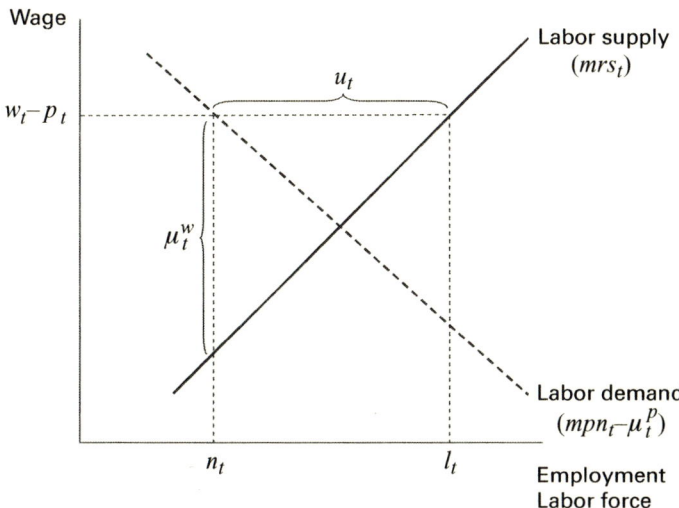

Figure 1.1
Wage markup and the unemployment rate

Figure 1.1 represents graphically this relationship, between the average wage markup and the unemployment rate, in a conventional labor market diagram. Notice that employment is demand-determined, given the wage.[5] The labor force is determined by the notional perfectly competitive labor supply. So the unemployment rate corresponds to the horizontal gap between the labor supply and labor demand schedules, at the level of the prevailing average real wage. The wage markup μ_t^w is represented in the figure by the vertical gap between labor supply and labor

---

5. Note that the demand schedule is given by the marginal product of labor (mpn_t, in logs) adjusted by the price markup (μ_t^p, also in logs). The firm behavior is discussed in the following section.

demand, at the level of current employment n_t. Given the linearity of both schedules, the ratio between the two gaps is constant and given by φ, the slope of the labor supply schedule.

I define the *natural* rate of unemployment, u_t^n, as the unemployment rate that would prevail in the absence of nominal wage rigidities. It follows from the assumption of a constant desired wage markup that such a natural rate is constant and given by

$$u^n = \frac{\mu^w}{\varphi}. \tag{1.13}$$

Equations (1.12) and (1.13) reveal fully the nature of unemployment in the present model. In particular, (1.13) shows that the presence of market power in the labor market, reflected in the wage markup $\mu^w > 0$, accounts for the existence of positive unemployment, even in the absence of wage rigidities. On the other hand, equation (1.12) implies that fluctuations in unemployment are a consequence of variations in the wage markup. Under the assumptions made above (consistent with those in EHL), wage markup variations are the result of nominal wage rigidities. The latter are, accordingly, the only source of unemployment fluctuations.

The conclusion above on the nature of unemployment fluctuations hinges critically on the assumption of a constant desired wage markup μ^w. In what follows, and given my objectives here, I will maintain that assumption. But it should be clear that the analysis above can be easily generalized to an environment in which the desired wage markup varies over time. In that case the natural rate of unemployment will fluctuate in response to variations in the desired markup. The fluctuations in actual unemployment will have two components: one associated with changes in the natural rate (driven by changes in the desired wage markup), and one driven by deviations of wage markups from their desired levels resulting from nominal wage rigidities. The interested reader can find an analysis of such a model allowing for variations in the desired wage markup in Galí, Smets, and Wouters (2011).

Finally, equations (1.8), (1.12), and (1.13) can be combined to derive a simple relation between wage inflation and the unemployment rate:

$$\pi_t^w = \beta E_t\{\pi_{t+1}^w\} - \lambda_w \varphi(u_t - u^n) \tag{1.14}$$

In Galí (2011a) I refer to this equation as the "New Keynesian wage Phillips curve," and provide some evidence in its support using postwar US data. Notice that in contrast to the Phillips original curve (Phillips 1958), which implied a simple static relation between wage inflation and unemployment, (1.14) is a forward-looking relation that treats wage inflation as a function of current and expected future unemployment rates. Also, whereas the original Phillips curve was a purely empirical relation, without any theoretical justification, (1.14) is derived from first principles, with its coefficients being a function of structural parameters.

1.2 Firms and Price Setting

The remaining components of the framework presented here follow closely standard versions of the New Keynesian model with staggered price and wage setting, so I will just summarize them briefly. Details and notation closely follow Galí (2008).

I assume a continuum of monopolistically competitive firms. Each firm produces a differentiated good $z \in [0, 1]$ using a production function

$$Y_t(z) = A_t N_t(z)^{1-\alpha},$$

where $N_t(z) \equiv \left(\int_0^1 N_t(i, z)^{1-(1/\epsilon_w)} di \right)^{\epsilon_w/(\epsilon_w-1)}$ is a CES index of the quantities of labor of different types employed by firm $z \in [0, 1]$ and A_t is an exogenous technology parameter. I assume that $a_t \equiv \log A_t$ follows an AR(1) process:

$$a_t = \rho_a a_{t-1} + \varepsilon_t^a,$$

where $\rho_a \in [0, 1]$ and ε_t^a is a white noise process with zero mean and variance σ_a^2.

Cost minimization, taking wages as given, implies the set of demand schedules $N_t(i, z) = (W_t(i)/W_t)^{-\epsilon_w} N_t(z)$, for all $i \in [0, 1]$ and $z \in [0, 1]$. The latter can be aggregated across firms to yield the labor demand schedules facing each union when setting the nominal wage, as used in the previous section.

Each firm resets the price of its good in any given period with a probability $1 - \theta_p$, independently of the time elapsed since it last reset its price. That probability is also independent across firms. As a result the (log) aggregate price level evolves over time according to the difference equation

$$p_t = \theta_p p_{t-1} + (1 - \theta_p) p_t^*, \tag{1.15}$$

where $p_t^* \equiv \log P_t^*$ is the (log) price newly set by firms adjusting the price in period t. When choosing that price P_t^*, each firm seeks to maximize its value subject to the sequence of demand constraints $Y_{t+k|t} = \left(P_t^*/P_{t+k} \right)^{-\epsilon_p} C_{t+k},$

for $k = 0, 1, 2, \ldots$, consistent with the households' optimality condition (1.2), where $Y_{t+k|t}$ denotes output at time $t + k$ of a firm that last reset its price in period t.

The resulting optimality condition is given by

$$\sum_{k=0}^{\infty} \theta_p^k \, E_t \left\{ Q_{t,t+k} \, Y_{t+k|t} \left(P_t^* - \mathcal{M}^p \Psi_{t+k|t} \right) \right\} = 0,$$

where $Q_{t,t+k} \equiv \beta^k (C_t/C_{t+k})(P_t/P_{t+k})$ is the relevant stochastic discount factor for nominal payoffs in period $t + k$, $\Psi_{t+k|t} \equiv W_{t+k}/[(1-\alpha) A_{t+k} N_{t+k|t}^{-\alpha}]$ is the marginal cost in period $t + k$ of producing quantity $Y_{t+k|t}$, and $\mathcal{M}^p \equiv \epsilon_p/(\epsilon_p - 1)$ is the desired or frictionless price markup over the marginal cost, meaning the price that would prevail if firms could reset their price every period ($\theta_p = 0$).

Log-linearization of the previous optimality condition around the zero inflation steady state yields

$$p_t^* = \mu^p + (1 - \beta \theta_p) \sum_{k=0}^{\infty} (\beta \theta_p)^k E_t \{\psi_{t+k|t}\}, \tag{1.16}$$

where $\mu^p \equiv \log \mathcal{M}^p$ and $\psi_{t+k|t} \equiv \log \Psi_{t+k|t}$. In words, firms adjusting their price in any given period choose the latter to equal the desired markup over a weighted average of current and future nominal marginal costs.

I define the *average* nominal marginal cost as $\Psi_t \equiv W_t/[(1-\alpha)(Y_t/N_t)]$. Taking logs and using the (first-order) approximate aggregate relation $y_t = a_t + (1-\alpha) n_t$ derived in the next section, it follows that

$$\psi_{t+k|t} = \psi_{t+k} + \alpha (n_{t+k|t} - n_{t+k})$$

$$= \psi_{t+k} - \frac{\alpha \epsilon_p}{(1-\alpha)} (p_t^* - p_{t+k}).$$

This result combined with (1.15) and (1.16) can be used to derive the price inflation equation

$$\pi_t^p = \beta E_t\{\pi_{t+1}^p\} - \lambda_p(\mu_t^p - \mu^p), \tag{1.17}$$

where $\pi_t^p \equiv p_t - p_{t-1}$ denotes price inflation, $\mu_t^p \equiv p_t - \psi_t$ is the *average* price markup and $\lambda_p \equiv [(1-\theta_p)(1-\beta\theta_p)/\theta_p]/[(1-\alpha)/(1-\alpha+\alpha\epsilon_p)]$. Thus price inflation is driven by current and expected deviations of average price markups from desired markups. Notice the symmetry between the price inflation equation (1.17) and its wage counterpart in (1.14).

Having derived the optimal wage and price setting rules and their implications for aggregate wage and price inflation, I turn to the model's market clearing conditions and a description of its equilibrium.

1.3   Equilibrium

Equilibrium in the goods market requires $C_t(z) = Y_t(z)$ for all $z \in [0,1]$. Define aggregate output as $Y_t \equiv \left(\int_0^1 Y_t(z)^{1-(1/\epsilon_p)} dz\right)^{\epsilon_p/(\epsilon_p-1)}$, so it follows that

$$C_t = Y_t.$$

Log-linearizing the consumer's Euler equation (1.3) and imposing the goods market-clearing condition, obtains

$$y_t = E_t\{y_{t+1}\} - (i_t - E_t\{\pi_{t+1}\} - \rho), \tag{1.18}$$

where $i_t \equiv -\log Q_t$ is the one-period nominal interest rate and $\rho \equiv -\log \beta$ is the time discount rate.

For the present purposes I define the *output gap*, $\tilde{y}_t$, as the (log) deviation between output and its *natural* (i.e., flexible

A Simple Model of Unemployment and Inflation Dynamics   21

price and wage) counterpart y_t^n, meaning $\tilde{y}_t \equiv y_t - y_t^n$. Then (1.18) can be rewritten in terms of the output gap as

$$\tilde{y}_t = E_t\{\tilde{y}_{t+1}\} - (i_t - E_t\{\pi_{t+1}\} - r_t^n), \tag{1.19}$$

where $r_t^n \equiv \rho + E_t\{\Delta y_{t+1}^n\}$ is the *natural* rate of interest.

The relation between aggregate employment and output is derived next. Equilibrium in the labor market implies that

$$\begin{aligned} N_t &= \int_0^1 \int_0^1 N_t(i,z)\, di\, dz \\ &= \int_0^1 N_t(z) \int_0^1 \frac{N_t(i,z)}{N_t(z)}\, di\, dz \\ &= \Delta_t^w \int_0^1 N_t(z)\, dz \\ &= \Delta_t^w \left(\frac{Y_t}{A_t}\right)^{1/(1-\alpha)} \int_0^1 \left(\frac{Y_t(z)}{Y_t}\right)^{1/(1-\alpha)} dz \\ &= \Delta_t^w \Delta_t^p \left(\frac{Y_t}{A_t}\right)^{1/(1-\alpha)}, \end{aligned} \tag{1.20}$$

where $\Delta_t^w \equiv \int_0^1 (W_t(i)/W_t)^{-\epsilon_w}\, di$ and $\Delta_t^p \equiv \int_0^1 (P_t(i)/P_t)^{-\epsilon_p/(1-\alpha)}\, di$. Variations in Δ_t^w and Δ_t^p around the steady state can be shown to be of second order (see appendix A). While those variations will play an important role in the discussion of welfare in chapter 4, they can be ignored in the present analysis of the linearized equilibrium conditions. Thus, and up to a first-order approximation,

$$y_t = a_t + (1-\alpha)n_t. \tag{1.21}$$

Letting $\omega_t \equiv w_t - p_t$ denote the (log) real wage, and defining the *wage gap* as $\tilde{\omega}_t \equiv \omega_t - \omega_t^n$, where ω_t^n is the natural wage (i.e., the equilibrium wage under flexible wages and prices), the price markup can be expressed, in deviation from its steady state value, as a function of the output and wage gaps:

$$\widehat{\mu}_t^p \equiv p_t - \psi_t - \mu^p$$
$$= \log(1-\alpha) + y_t - n_t - \omega_t - \mu^p$$
$$= -\left(\frac{\alpha}{1-\alpha}\right)\widetilde{y}_t - \widetilde{\omega}_t.$$

Substituting the latter expression into the price inflation equation yields

$$\pi_t^p = \beta E_t\{\pi_{t+1}^p\} + \kappa_p \widetilde{y}_t + \lambda_p \widetilde{\omega}_t, \qquad (1.22)$$

where $\kappa_p \equiv \lambda_p[\alpha/(1-\alpha)]$.

Similarly, the definition of the (log) wage markup, combined with the goods market-clearing condition, yields

$$\widehat{\mu}_t^w \equiv \omega_t - (y_t + \varphi n_t + \xi_t) - \mu^w$$
$$= \widetilde{\omega}_t - \left(1 + \frac{\varphi}{1-\alpha}\right)\widetilde{y}_t. \qquad (1.23)$$

This result allows the wage inflation equation to be written as

$$\pi_t^w = \beta E_t\{\pi_{t+1}^w\} + \kappa_w \widetilde{y}_t - \lambda_w \widetilde{\omega}_t, \qquad (1.24)$$

where $\kappa_w \equiv \lambda_w\{1 + [\varphi/(1-\alpha)]\}$.

Combining (1.12) and (1.23), I can derive the following relation between the unemployment rate and the output and wage gaps as:

$$\varphi \widehat{u}_t = \widetilde{\omega}_t - \left(1 + \frac{\varphi}{1-\alpha}\right)\widetilde{y}_t. \qquad (1.25)$$

A Simple Model of Unemployment and Inflation Dynamics

Note also that the following identity linking the wage gap, price inflation, and wage inflation holds:

$$\tilde{\omega}_t = \tilde{\omega}_{t-1} + \pi_t^w - \pi_t^p - \Delta \omega_t^n. \tag{1.26}$$

I close the model by assuming a Taylor-type interest rate rule of the form

$$i_t = \rho + \phi_\pi \pi_t^p + \phi_y \widehat{y}_t + v_t, \tag{1.27}$$

where $\widehat{y}_t \equiv y_t - y$ is the log deviation of output from steady state, and v_t is an exogenous monetary policy component, which is assumed to follow an AR(1) process:

$$v_t = \rho_v v_{t-1} + \varepsilon_t^v,$$

where $\rho_v \in [0, 1]$ and ε_t^v is a white noise process with zero mean and variance σ_v^2.

Equations (1.19), (1.22), (1.24), (1.25), (1.26), and (1.27) describe the equilibrium dynamics for the output gap, the wage gap, price and wage inflation, the unemployment rate, and the nominal interest rate, as a function of the monetary policy shock v_t, the natural wage ω_t^n and the natural interest rate r_t^n. The last two variables are in turn a function of the underlying real shocks (technology and preference), which can be easily derived by imposing $\mu_t^w = \mu^w$ and $\mu^p = \mu^p$ for all t in the equilibrium above. Some straightforward algebra yields the following expressions for the natural values of the wage, output and interest rate:

$$\omega_t^n = a_t + \left(\frac{\alpha}{1+\varphi}\right)\xi_t,$$

$$y_t^n = a_t - \left(\frac{1-\alpha}{1+\varphi}\right)\xi_t,$$

and

$$r_t^n = \rho + E_t\{\Delta a_{t+1}\} - \left(\frac{1-\alpha}{1+\varphi}\right) E_t\{\Delta \xi_{t+1}\}$$

$$= \rho - (1-\rho_a)a_t + \frac{(1-\alpha)(1-\rho_\xi)}{1+\varphi}\xi_t.$$

Note that the second equality makes use of the assumptions on the processes followed by a_t and ξ_t.

1.4 Nominal Wage Rigidities and Unemployment Fluctuations: Some Simulations

This section reports the impulse responses and statistical properties of some key macro variables for a calibrated version of the model developed in section 1.3. The ultimate goal of the exercise is to assess the potential role played by nominal wage rigidities as a source of unemployment fluctuations in response to different types of shocks. In doing so, it is important to recognize the model's inherent limitations to provide a full account of the observed behavior of macro variables, since it lacks many of the bells and whistles found in medium-scale DSGE models (habit formation, capital accumulation, indexation, etc.). The advantage, nevertheless lies in the transparency associated with the model's simplicity and its focus on the key elements behind the issue of interest.

1.4.1 Calibration

Table 1.1 reports the values assumed for the different parameters in the baseline calibration. Each period is assumed to correspond to a quarter. The setting chosen for many of the parameters is standard. The discount factor β is set to 0.99.

Table 1.1
Baseline Calibration

Parameter	Description	Value
φ	Curvature of labor disutility	5
ϵ_w	Elasticity of substitution among labor types	4.52
ϵ_p	Elasticity of substitution among goods	9
θ_p	Calvo index of price rigidities	0.75
θ_w	Calvo index of wage rigidities	0.75
α	Decreasing returns to labor	1/4
ϕ_p	Inflation coefficient in policy rule	1.5
ϕ_y	Output coefficient in policy rule	0.125
β	Discount factor	0.99

Parameter α, measuring the degree of decreasing returns to labor, is set to 1/4. The elasticity of substitution among goods, ϵ_p, is set to 9, implying a steady state price markup of 12.5 percent. Together with the calibration of α, this is consistent with a steady state labor income share of 2/3, which is close to the average labor income share observed in the US and the euro area. I assume baseline values for θ_p and θ_w, the Calvo indexes of price and wage rigidities, of 3/4, which implies an average duration of price and wage contracts of one year in a way consistent with much of the micro evidence.[6]

Note that relative to the standard New Keynesian model, the introduction of unemployment poses some discipline on the calibration of φ (the inverse Frisch elasticity of labor supply) and ϵ_w (the elasticity of substitution among labor types in production). The reason is that the average wage

---

6. See, for example, Nakamura and Steinsson (2008) and Taylor (1999a).

markup (itself a function of ϵ_w) is tied to the natural rate of unemployment through the relation $\mathcal{M}^w \equiv \epsilon_w/(\epsilon_w - 1) = \exp\{\varphi u^n\}$. Assuming baseline values $\varphi = 5$ (i.e., a Frisch elasticity of 0.2) and $u^n = 0.05$ (consistent with an average unemployment rate of 5 percent) implies $\epsilon_w = 4.52$, which in turn is associated with an average wage markup of 28 percent.

The choice of coefficients for the interest rate rule follows Taylor (1993); namely I set $\phi_p = 1.5$ and $\phi_y = 0.5/4 = 0.125$. Finally, I choose a baseline value of 0.9 for the autoregressive coefficients of the three driving processes ($\rho_a = \rho_\xi = \rho_v = 0.9$).

1.4.2 Impulse Responses and Conditional Second Moments

Figures 1.2 to 1.4 show the dynamic responses of six macro variables (output, unemployment, employment, labor force, the real wage, and inflation) to the three exogenous shocks considered in the model above—technology, monetary, and labor supply shocks—under the baseline calibration.

Figure 1.2 displays the impulse responses to a 1 percent increase in the technology parameter. Notice that output rises and inflation declines, as would be expected in response to such a shock. However, and in contrast with the predictions of a standard search and matching model, the unemployment rate increases, and substantially so, in response to an improvement in technology. That increase is largely the result of a drop in employment, hardly muted by the small decline in the labor force. That prediction of the model regarding the response of employment and unemployment to a technology shock is consistent with much of the empirical evidence found in the literature, even though that evidence is generally ignored by economists

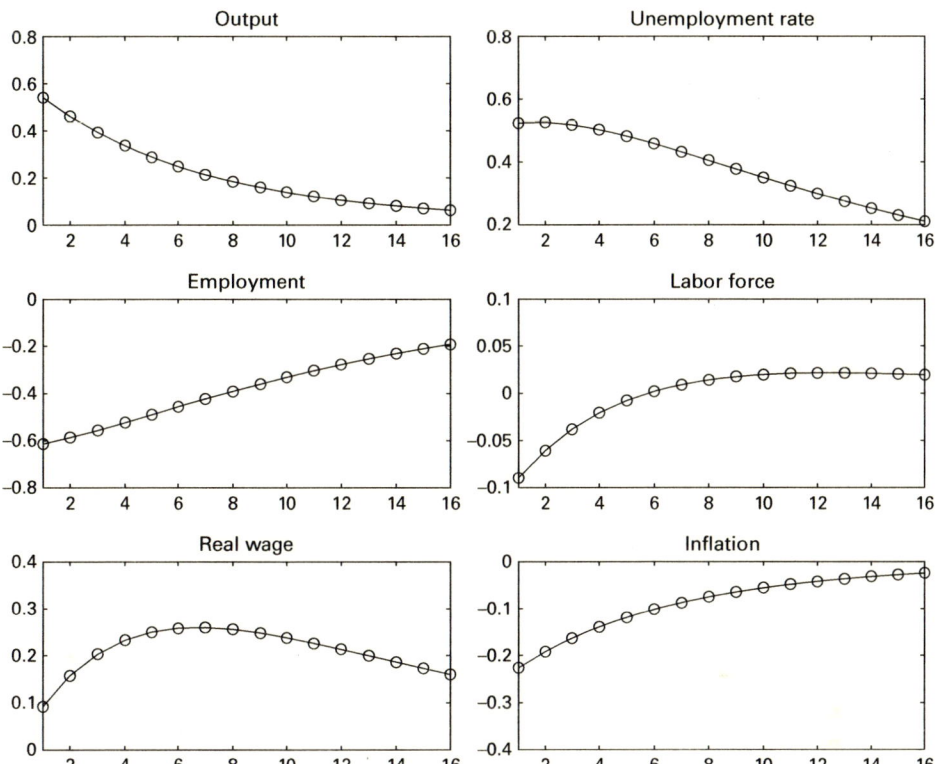

Figure 1.2
Dynamic responses to a technology shock

working with search and matching models.[7] Notice also that the real wage rises gradually, a natural consequence of the

---

7. See Galí (1999), Basu, Fernald, and Kimball (2006), Francis and Ramey (2005), and Galí and Rabanal (2004), among others, for evidence of a decline in labor input, with a focus on hours rather than employment. Evidence of a short run rise in unemployment in response to a positive supply shock can also be found in Blanchard and Quah (1989) and, more recently, in Barnichon (2008).

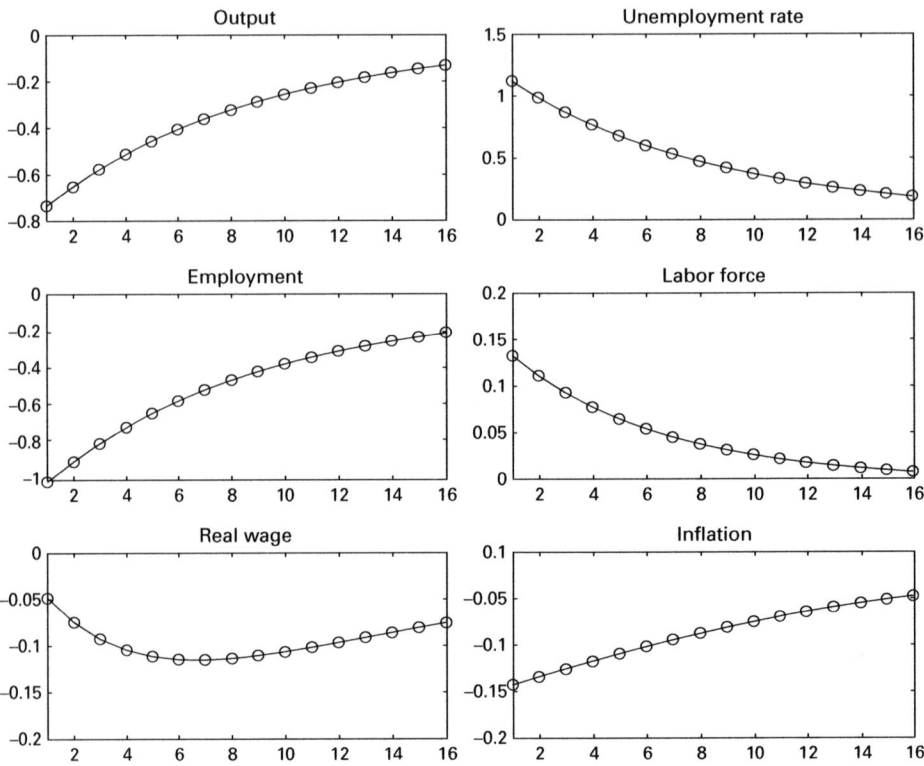

Figure 1.3
Dynamic responses to a monetary shock

existence of nominal wage rigidities. The increase in real wages is, however, exclusively the result of a decline in the price level, since the average nominal wage (not shown) goes down due to the rise in unemployment (this is an implication of equation 1.14).

Figure 1.3 displays the responses to a monetary policy shock, one that takes the form of a 25 basis point increase

A Simple Model of Unemployment and Inflation Dynamics

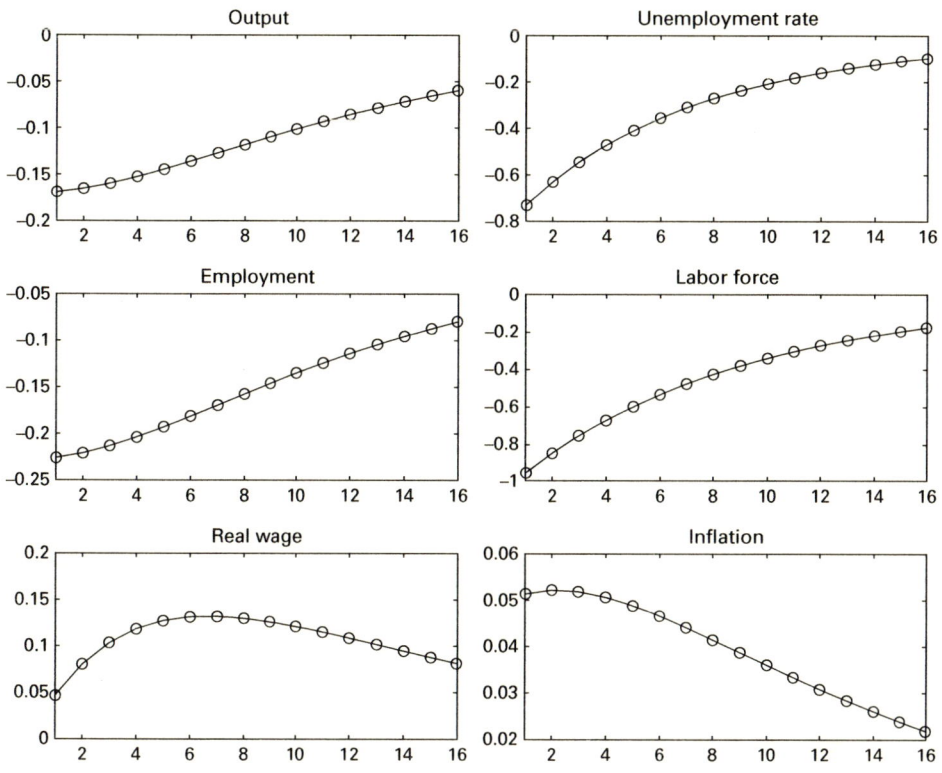

Figure 1.4
Dynamic responses to a labor supply shock

in v_t. In the absence of an endogenous policy response, that increase would lead to a 1 percentage point rise in the (annualized) nominal rate. As the figure makes clear, both output and employment decline substantially in response to the tightening of monetary policy, due to the contraction in consumption (not shown) resulting from the interest rate hike. The labor force tends to rise (due to the negative wealth effect), but only by a small amount.[8] As a result the unemployment rate increases by more than one percentage point. Note also that price inflation moves procyclically, while the real wage declines as a result of the downward pressure of unemployment on nominal wages.

Figure 1.4 shows the responses to a labor supply shock, corresponding to a 5 percent increase in ξ_t. Given the setting for parameter φ that increase is consistent with a 1 percent contraction in the labor force, conditional on the real wage and consumption remaining unchanged. Note that the unemployment rate declines substantially as a result of the drop in the labor force, making upward pressure on wages, and hence on price inflation. The policy rule leads the central bank to raise interest rates, leading to a decline in aggregate demand, output, and employment. Notice however, that the changes in all these variables are relative small relative to the variation in the labor force and the unemployment rate. In particular, the decline in employment offsets less than one-fourth of the decline in the labor force.

The first two panels of table 1.2 report the standard deviations (relative to GDP) and the correlations with GDP of the unemployment rate, employment, the labor force, the real wage and inflation, based on quarterly data for both the US and the euro area.[9] The sample period is 1948Q1 to 2009Q4 for the United States and 1970Q1 to 2009Q4 for

---

8. Although small, the countercyclical response of the labor force to a monetary shock appears to be at odds with the empirical evidence reported in Christiano, Trabandt, and Walentin (2010). Galí, Smets, and Wouters (2011) modify the household's utility function along the lines of Jaimovich and Rebelo (2009), and show that a specification of the latter consistent with small wealth effects implies a procyclical (and small) response of the labor force to a monetary shock, in a way consistent with the evidence.

9. Data for the United States are from the Haver database. Data for the euro area are from the Area Wide Model dataset (update 9), as first documented

Table 1.2
Second Moments: Model and Data Compared

	United States		Euro Area		Technology		Monetary		Labor Supply	
	$\frac{\sigma(x)}{\sigma(y)}$	$\rho(x,y)$	$\frac{\sigma(x)}{\sigma(y)}$	$\rho(x,y)$	$\frac{\sigma(x)}{\sigma(y)}$	$\rho(x,y)$	$\frac{\sigma(x)}{\sigma(y)}$	$\rho(x,y)$	$\frac{\sigma(x)}{\sigma(y)}$	$\rho(x,y)$
Unemployment	0.48	−0.88	0.41	−0.68	1.30	0.96	1.68	−0.99	4.42	0.95
Employment	0.63	0.81	0.62	0.78	1.44	−0.98	1.49	0.99	1.49	0.99
Labor force	0.23	0.28	0.32	0.56	0.17	−0.92	0.17	−0.98	5.87	0.97
Real wage	0.59	0.13	0.68	0.27	0.38	0.53	0.15	0.57	0.87	−0.75
Inflation	0.34	0.35	0.38	0.34	0.40	−0.99	0.20	0.99	0.31	−0.99

the euro area. Employment, the labor force, and GDP are normalized by working age population and, together with the real wage, are expressed in natural logarithms. All variables are detrended using a Hodrick–Prescott filter with a smoothing parameter of 1600. Many of the stylized facts shown in table 1.2 are well known and common to both the U.S. and the euro area. Notice that employment is substantially more volatile than the labor force, while the volatility of the unemployment rate lies somewhere in between. All three variables are far less volatile than GDP. The real wage is also shown to be substantially less volatile than GDP. Turning to the correlation with GDP, we see that the unemployment rate is highly countercyclical in both economies. Employment and the labor force are, however, procyclical, although the latter is only moderately so, especially in the United States. The real wage is only mildly positively

---

in Fagan, Henry, and Mestre (2001). Both sources define inflation by the percent change in the consumer price index. The wage measure used corresponds to compensation per hour in the nonfarm business sector for the United States and to the "wage per head" variable in the AWM dataset for the euro area. The real wage measure is constructed as the ratio of the wage to the consumer price index in both cases.

correlated with GDP, more so in the euro area. Price inflation is mildly procyclical in both economies.

The remaining panels in table 1.2 show the corresponding statistics generated by the calibrated model, conditional on each of the three shocks, and after application of the same HP filter used on the data. In a way consistent with the impulse responses above, technology shocks can be seen to generate countercyclical employment and labor force (and a procyclical unemployment rate). Furthermore the implied relative volatilities of the unemployment rate and employment are far larger than those observed in the (raw) data. The real wage is smooth relative to output and mildly procyclical, but inflation is highly countercyclical.

The patterns generated by monetary shocks (which can be viewed as a stand-in for a generic aggregate demand shock) are shown in the next panel. As in the data, unemployment is now highly countercyclical and employment highly procyclical, but both are too variable relative to output. The labor force, however, is very smooth like in the data, but countercyclical. The real wage is less volatile than output, and mildly procyclical, patterns that are also observed in the unconditional statistics. Price inflation is also less volatile than output, but highly procyclical, in response to monetary shocks.

The last panel reports the second moments generated by labor supply shocks. Not surprisingly, the most noticeable feature is the high relative volatility and procyclicality of the labor force, properties that are inherited by the unemployment rate. The latter variable, as seen in the impulse responses moves procyclically, while both the real wage and inflation are highly countercyclical (all in contrast with the unconditional statistics).

A Simple Model of Unemployment and Inflation Dynamics 33

From the previous analysis, it seems clear that none of the shocks considered are capable, when considered in isolation, of generating the patterns of relative volatilities and correlations observed in the data. Monetary shocks, however, come somewhat closer in that they generate both a countercyclical unemployment rate and a procyclical employment, two central features of cyclical fluctuations in industrialized economies.

1.4.3 Wage Rigidities and the Volatility and Persistence of Unemployment

In the model developed above, unemployment fluctuations are the result of nominal wage rigidities. In the absence of the latter, the unemployment rate would be constant at a level proportional to the desired wage markup. So at this point I will explore in more depth the connection between wage rigidities and the properties of unemployment fluctuations. For the sake of concreteness, I will restrict the discussion to fluctuations driven by monetary shocks. As shown in the previous subsection, monetary shocks are the only shocks (of the three considered above) that generate a countercyclical unemployment rate in the model's baseline calibration. Again, monetary shocks could be viewed as a stand-in for other aggregate demand shocks (e.g., shocks to the discount rate).

Table 1.3 reports measures of volatility, persistence and cyclicality of unemployment, conditioned on monetary policy shocks, for alternative configurations of values for the degree of wage stickiness, θ_w, and the autoregressive coefficient of the shock process, ρ_v. I choose the standard deviation of the unemployment rate as a measure of unemployment volatility, and normalize the variance of the shock

Table 1.3
Wage Rigidities and Unemployment Fluctuations

	Volatility			Persistence			Cyclicality		
θ_w :	0.1	0.5	0.75	0.1	0.5	0.75	0.1	0.5	0.75
$\rho_v = 0.0$	0.18	0.22	0.23	−0.16	−0.08	−0.07	−0.99	−1.0	−1.0
$\rho_v = 0.5$	0.24	0.39	0.42	0.20	0.34	0.37	−0.98	−0.99	−1.0
$\rho_v = 0.9$	0.15	0.54	1.0	0.40	0.62	0.68	−0.92	−0.99	−1.0

σ_v^2 so that, under the baseline calibration ($\theta_w = 0.75$, $\rho_v = 0.9$), the standard deviation of the unemployment rate equals one.[10] The first-order autocorrelation of the unemployment rate is reported as a measure of persistence, and the correlation with output is used as a measure of cyclicality. The question I pose here is: To what extent does the degree of nominal rigidities influence the volatility, persistence and cyclicality of the unemployment rate?

The statistics reported in table 1.3 help answer that question. First, notice that unemployment *volatility* increases with the degree of nominal wage rigidities θ_w, for any given degree of persistence of the shock. This can be explained by the fact that wage rigidities are the only source of unemployment fluctuations in the model. Other things equal, more rigid wages should imply more volatile unemployment. Observe also that unemployment volatility is increasing in the persistence of the monetary shock when wages are sufficiently rigid. When $\theta_w = 0.1$, however, the relation is no longer monotonic.

---

10. I could have instead matched an arbitrary (absolute) standard deviation of the unemployment rate by adjusting the volatility of the exogenous shock, but the calibration of such a parameter would always be controversial.

As to the implied *persistence* of the unemployment rate, the second panel of table 1.3 shows how the autocorrelation of the latter is increasing in the degree of nominal wage rigidities (and, less surprisingly, in the persistence of the shock). Notice that the autocorrelation always remains below the autocorrelation of the shock process, and substantially so when wages are relatively flexible. Under the baseline calibration the persistence of the unemployment rate is pretty strong (0.68), although still below the persistence observed in the data: the autocorrelation of the (HP-detrended) unemployment rate is as high 0.90 in the United States and 0.92 in the euro area. It is also interesting that for sufficiently low values of ρ_v, the unemployment rate becomes negatively serially correlated, a property that it inherits from employment.

The third panel of table 1.3 shows the correlation between the unemployment rate and output. It is minus one or close to minus one for all calibrations. The strong countercyclicality of unemployment in response of monetary shocks thus seems to be a robust feature of the model, independently of the degree of wage stickiness and the persistence of those shocks.

The simplicity of the underlying model notwithstanding, the simulation findings reported above yield at least one clear lesson: that realistic nominal wage rigidities may alone be a significant source of unemployment fluctuations, of size and persistence comparable to those found in postwar US and euro area data. More research is thus warranted to determine the extent to which factors *other than wage rigidities* (e.g., search frictions) are a significant source of unemployment variations. As discussed above, changes in natural wage markups may be one such source. The estimates of a version of the model above allowing for stochastic variations in natural wage markups, found in Galí, Smets, and Wouters (2011), imply that as much as one-third of the forecast error variance of unemployment at a ten-year horizon is due to such shocks. However, recent work by Shimer (2005, 2010), Hall (2005), Blanchard and Galí (2010), and Galí (2011), among others, suggests that labor market frictions are not likely to be an important source of unemployment fluctuations, absent wage rigidities of some sort. Furthermore the observed pattern of unemployment over time points to the presence of nonnegligible low-frequency movements, especially in the euro area. To the extent that those movements are unrelated to the presence of nominal wage rigidities, they should be interpreted as reflecting changes in the natural rate of unemployment. In the context of the model above, those changes would reflect variations in the natural (or desired) wage markup resulting from changes in workers' market power. Of course, alternative unemployment models could point to other factors as an explanation for those low-frequency movements.

Given the use of HP-filtered data in the analysis, I have abstracted from low frequency movements in the unemployment rate (and also in other variables). But, for a more thorough understanding of unemployment and its determinants, such movements should be taken into account. Future research should thus provide some guidance as to the importance of factors other than nominal wage rigidities, and incorporate them in current monetary DSGE models.

2 Unemployment, the Output Gap, and the Welfare Costs of Economic Fluctuations

The instability associated with business cycles has traditionally been regarded as one of the unpleasant sides of capitalism, and a price society has to pay in order to reap the longer term benefits of free enterprise and market-driven innovation. At least since Keynes (1936), recessions have been viewed as periods in which the economy operates below the efficient level of activity and resource utilization. Expansions, in contrast, bring the economy close to the efficient level. That interpretation of the ups-and-downs in business activity has underpinned the adoption of stabilization policies aimed at dampening (if not fully eliminating) economic downturns.

That traditional view has not remained unchallenged. Thus, at the other extreme of the spectrum, early incarnations of the real business cycle (RBC) theory (e.g., Kydland and Prescott 1982; Prescott 1986) proposed an interpretation of cyclical fluctuations as the economy's efficient response to a variety of exogenous disturbances. Under the RBC view, stabilization policies, no matter how well intentioned, are likely to be counterproductive and lead to a decline in utility.[1]

A key explanation for the coexistence of such discrepant views is the *unobservability* of the efficient level of output. That unobservability renders the construction of measures of the gap between output and its efficient benchmark a nontrivial enterprise. Thus, and as stressed by Galí and Gertler (1999) and Galí (2003), among others, traditional measures of slack (e.g., detrended log GDP) are likely to be poor proxies of the "true" output gap. The reason is that those measures take the reference level of output to be a smooth function of time that can be approximated by a conventional statistical trend. In contrast, modern business cycle theory implies that the efficient level of output can display potentially large short-run fluctuations in response to all kinds of shocks. The latter observation is arguably one of the main lessons of RBC theory.

In this chapter, I revisit the connection between economic fluctuations and efficiency using the New Keynesian framework, as exemplified by the model developed in chapter 1. The equilibrium allocation in that model is generally inefficient as a consequence of several imperfections embedded in it. Thus the market power enjoyed by firms and workers tends to bring about an inefficiently low level of activity, even in the absence of shocks and fluctuations. In addition the presence of nominal rigidities leads to endogenous variations in price and wage markups and, as a result, changes over time in the "distance" between the actual equilibrium allocation and its efficient counterpart. Finally, the

---

1. In the words of Prescott (1986, p. 39): "The policy implication of this research is that costly efforts at stabilization are likely to be counterproductive. Economic fluctuations are optimal responses to uncertainty in the rate of technological change."

assumption of staggered price and wage setting leads to a dispersion in prices and wages unwarranted by differences in fundamentals, with a consequent misallocation of resources across firms and workers. I focus on the first two sources of inefficiency, leaving the discussion of the welfare consequences of nominal dispersion for the following chapter.

I first develop a measure of the *output gap*, consistent with the model developed in chapter 1. Under certain assumptions the measure of the output gap proposed here provides an index of the economy's slack relative to the first-best allocation, and can thus be used to evaluate the magnitude and cyclical properties of that "efficiency gap."[2] Then I analyze the implications for welfare of the output gap and its fluctuations, by computing a measure of the associated deadweight losses and analyzing its changes over time. In both exercises I use quarterly data for the United States and for the euro area.

In spirit, as well as in some details, the analysis below builds heavily on my earlier research on "gaps" with Mark Gertler and David López-Salido (Galí, Gertler, and López-Salido 2007; henceforth, GGL).[3] In that work we sought to overcome the unobservability problem mentioned above

---

2. Justiniano and Primiceri (2008) and Sala, Söderström, and Trigari (2010) are examples of recent work aiming to estimate and analyze the properties of the output gap using a full-fledged DSGE model with a richer structure than the framework used here, but without exploiting the information contained in the unemployment data. Galí, Smets, and Wouters (2011) perform a similar analysis but with a version of the Smets–Wouters (2007) model, estimated using unemployment data, and exploiting the relation between the latter and the average wage markup emphasized by the present framework.

3. See also Mulligan (2002) and Chari, Kehoe, and McGrattan (2007) for related analyses.

by using the distance between the (log) marginal rate of substitution (between consumption and work hours) and the (log) marginal product of labor as a measure of the extent of underutilization of resources relative to first best. Formally, and using the notation of the model in chapter 1, in GGL we defined the inefficiency gap as[4]

$$gap_t = mrs_t - mpn_t$$
$$= (c_t + \varphi n_t + \xi_t) - (y_t - n_t + \log(1 - \alpha)). \tag{2.1}$$

Unfortunately, and as made clear by (2.1), the construction of the GGL gap also runs into a hurdle of its own, namely the unobservability of the preference shifter ξ_t, which affects the marginal rate of substitution. Assuming away the existence of a preference shifter does not seem satisfactory. Low-frequency changes in the labor force due to demographic and sociological factors are likely to be captured by movements in that shifter. Still, and as suggested by the work of Shapiro and Watson (1988) and Hall (1997), among others, preference shocks of the sort that would be captured by ξ_t may have played a nonnegligible role as a source of short-run fluctuations.

In GGL we dealt with that unobservability problem by assuming that the preference shifter $\{\xi_t\}$ evolves smoothly over time, and proxying the gap_t variable accordingly by detrending its "observable" component, $gap_t - \xi_t = (c_t + \varphi n_t) - (y_t - n_t)$, with a polynomial function of time. The resulting gap measure was shown to be highly procyclical, and to display a high positive correlation with traditional measures of economic slack (e.g., detrended GDP).

---

4. Under some assumptions (satisfied by the model developed in chapter 1), the GGL gap is proportional to the gap between actual output and its efficient counterpart.

The approach pursued here exploits instead the connection between the wage markup and the unemployment rate uncovered in chapter 1 to develop a measure of the output gap that is a function of observable variables and that can accommodate arbitrary variations at all frequencies in the preference shifter $\{\xi_t\}$.

2.1 Unemployment Fluctuations and the Output Gap

Some of the key relations from the model developed in chapter 1 to derive an exact expression for the gap between output and its efficient counterpart. Recall that the average price markup, expressed in levels, can be written as

$$\mathcal{M}_t^p = \frac{(1-\alpha)(Y_t/N_t)}{W_t/P_t}. \tag{2.2}$$

Similarly the average wage markup is given by

$$\mathcal{M}_t^w = \frac{W_t/P_t}{\chi_t C_t N_t^\varphi}. \tag{2.3}$$

Combining both definitions, and using the goods market-clearing condition, $C_t = Y_t$, we derive the following expression for equilibrium employment:

$$N_t = \left(\frac{1-\alpha}{\mathcal{M}_t \chi_t}\right)^{1/(1+\varphi)}, \tag{2.4}$$

where $\mathcal{M}_t \equiv \mathcal{M}_t^p \mathcal{M}_t^w \geq 1$ is a combined measure of wage and price markups, which I refer to as the *composite markup*, for short. Thus, under the assumptions of chapter 1, we see that equilibrium employment varies as a result of shocks to preferences, as well as in response to any other shocks but only to the extent that the latter have an impact on price and wage markups (as they will generally do when prices and/or wages are sticky).

Plugging (2.4) into (1.20) yields the following expression for aggregate output:

$$Y_t = \frac{A_t}{\Delta_t^{1-\alpha}} \left(\frac{1-\alpha}{\mathcal{M}_t \chi_t} \right)^{(1-\alpha)/(1+\varphi)}, \tag{2.5}$$

where $\Delta_t \equiv \Delta_t^w \Delta_t^p \geq 1$ is an index of nominal dispersion, which combines the measures of price and wage dispersion defined in chapter 1. Thus both output and employment are decreasing in the preference shifter and in the composite markup. In addition output is increasing in technology and decreasing in the combined nominal dispersion measure.

I define the *efficient* levels of output and employment, denoted by Y_t^e and N_t^e, as those corresponding to the equilibrium levels for those variables under perfectly competitive goods and labor markets ($\mathcal{M}_t = 1$, for all t), and fully flexible wages and prices ($\Delta_t = 1$, for all t). Thus we have

$$N_t^e = \left(\frac{1-\alpha}{\chi_t} \right)^{1/(1+\varphi)} \tag{2.6}$$

and

$$Y_t^e = A_t \left(\frac{1-\alpha}{\chi_t} \right)^{(1-\alpha)(1+\varphi)}. \tag{2.7}$$

Finally, I define the *welfare-relevant output gap*, denoted by x_t, as the log deviation between output and its efficient counterpart, namely $x_t \equiv y_t - y_t^e$. As shown in appendix A, the nominal dispersion term Δ_t is of second order. This allows the welfare-relevant output gap to be written, up to a first-order approximation, as

$$x_t = -\left(\frac{1-\alpha}{1+\varphi} \right) (\mu_t^p + \mu_t^w), \tag{2.8}$$

that is, the welfare-relevant output gap is proportional to the (log) composite markup.

Notice that the *natural* level of output can be written as

$$Y_t^n = A_t \left(\frac{1-\alpha}{\mathcal{M}\chi_t}\right)^{(1-\alpha)/(1+\varphi)}$$

It follows that

$$x_t = \tilde{y}_t + y_t^n - y_t^e$$
$$= \tilde{y}_t - \left(\frac{1-\alpha}{1+\varphi}\right)\mu.$$

In words, the two output gap variables are identical except for a constant additive term proportional to the steady state composite markup. For the purposes of the present section, however, I will focus on x_t, while referring to it as the output gap, for convenience.

Next I show how one can express the output gap in terms of observables by using two key relations. The first relation, linking the average wage markup to the unemployment rate, was derived in chapter 1, and is rewritten here for convenience:

$$\mu_t^w = \varphi u_t. \tag{2.9}$$

The second relation links the average price markup to the labor income share:

$$\mu_t^p \equiv p_t - \psi_t$$
$$= p_t - (w_t - (y_t - n_t + \log(1-\alpha)))$$
$$= \log(1-\alpha) - s_t, \tag{2.10}$$

where $s_t \equiv (w_t + n_t) - (p_t + y_t)$ is the (log) labor income share, an observable variable. The previous relation has been exploited in the past to study the cyclical properties of the average price markup (e.g., Rotemberg and Woodford 1999b) or to estimate inflation equation (1.17) (e.g., Galí and Gertler 1999; Sbordone 2002).

Combining (2.8) with (2.9) and (2.10) yields the following expression for the output gap as a function of observable variables:

$$x_t = \left(\frac{1-\alpha}{1+\varphi}\right)(s_t - \varphi u_t - \log(1-\alpha)). \tag{2.11}$$

Thus, given values for parameters α and φ, a time series for the output gap can be constructed using readily available data on the unemployment rate and the labor income share. I do so next, using both US and euro area data.

For the United States I use National Income Accounts data to construct the labor income share as the sum of "compensation of employees" and a fraction of "proprietors' income," divided by nominal GDP. Following common practice, proprietor's income is allocated to labor income in proportion to the latter's weight in total income minus proprietor's income. For the euro area, I do not have data on proprietor's income, so I just use compensation of employees divided by GDP, with both series being drawn from the AWM database. Unless otherwise noted, I use the settings for parameters α and φ assumed in the baseline calibration of the model of chapter 1, namely $\alpha = 0.25$ and $\varphi = 5$.

Figures 2.1 and 2.2 display the implied output gap series for the United States and the euro area, respectively. The shaded areas highlight the recession episodes, as dated by the NBER and the CEPR. The output gap measures are seen to display nontrivial fluctuations. For the United States the output gap fluctuates between -4 and -10 percent, whereas in the euro area the range of fluctuations lies between -5

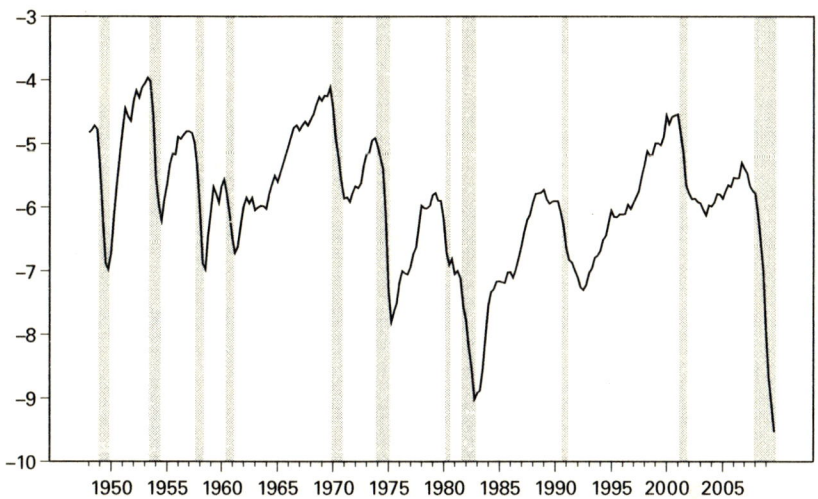

Figure 2.1
US output gap

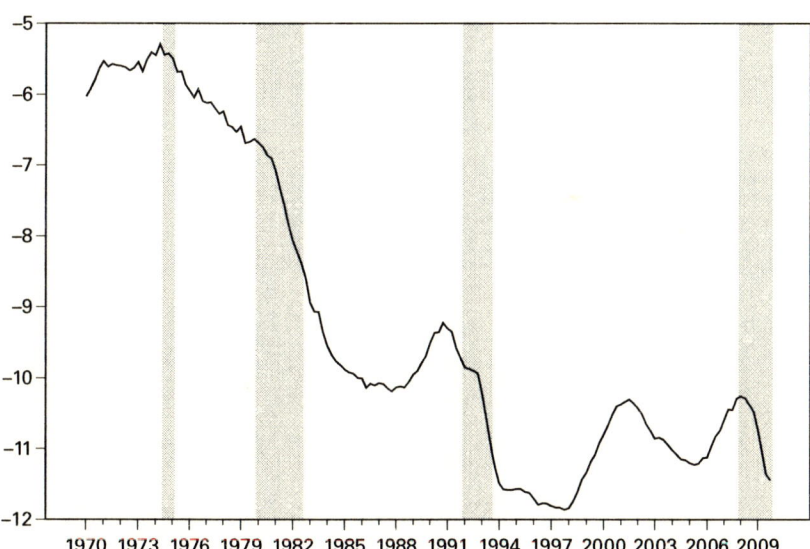

Figure 2.2
Euro area output gap

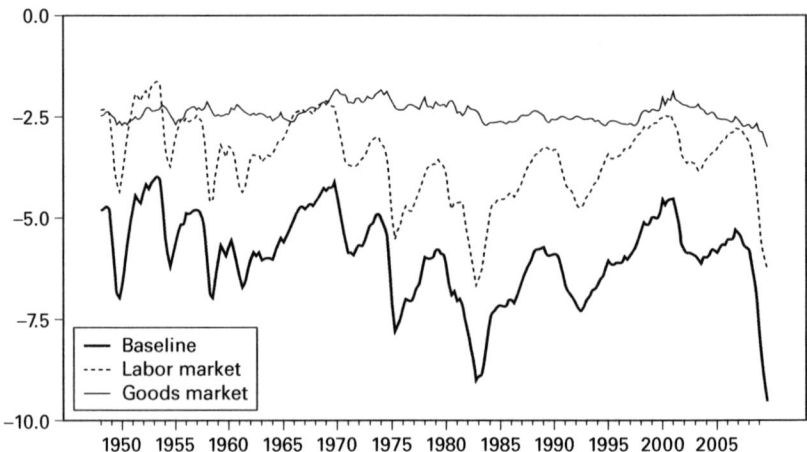

Figure 2.3
US output gap and its components

and −12 percent. Note also that the US output gap appears to be largely stationary, but in the euro area its behavior shows a markedly nonstationary pattern. In both economies, however, the output gap declines noticeably during recessions. That observation, also uncovered in GGL, is consistent with the Keynesian interpretation of recessions as periods in which the distance from the efficient level of activity rises.

Figure 2.3 and 2.4 plot the US and euro area output gaps together with their components. The first component, given by $x_t^w \equiv -[(1-\alpha)\varphi/(1+\varphi)]u_t$, captures the shortfall in output resulting from market power and wage rigidities in the labor market. The second component, defined by $x_t^p \equiv [(1-\alpha)/(1+\varphi)]/(s_t - \log(1-\alpha))$, reflects the distortions originating in the goods market, resulting from firms' market power and the stickiness of prices. Figure 2.3 shows that the labor market component is the dominant

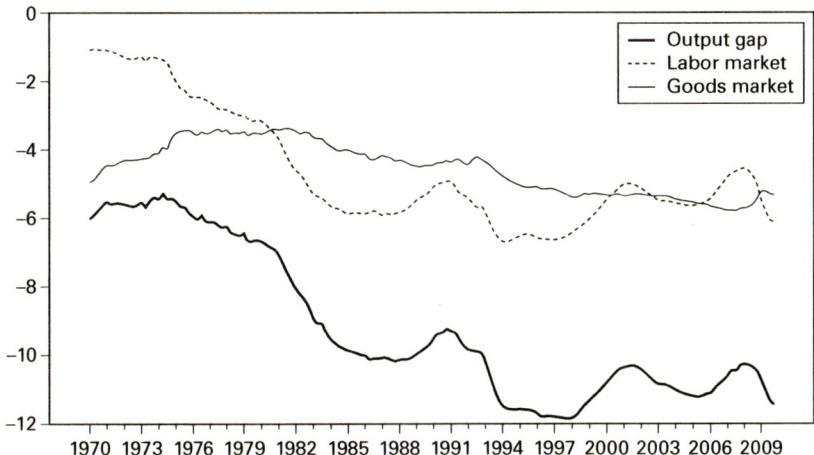

Figure 2.4
Euro area output gap and its components

source of cyclical variations in the US output gap, with the goods market component playing a negligible role. A similar picture emerges for the euro area (see Figure 2.4), though in this case the goods market component also displays a pronounced trend downward, which is reflected in the output gap measure.

Figures 2.5 and 2.6 display again the US and euro area output gaps, together with a conventional measure of the cyclical component of GDP, namely, HP-detrended (log) GDP.[5] For the United States the correlation between the two series is positive and high, but far from unity (0.58), suggesting that conventional output gap measures may provide a reasonable but still imperfect approximation to the

---

5. Following convention in the literature, I use a smoothing parameter of 1600.

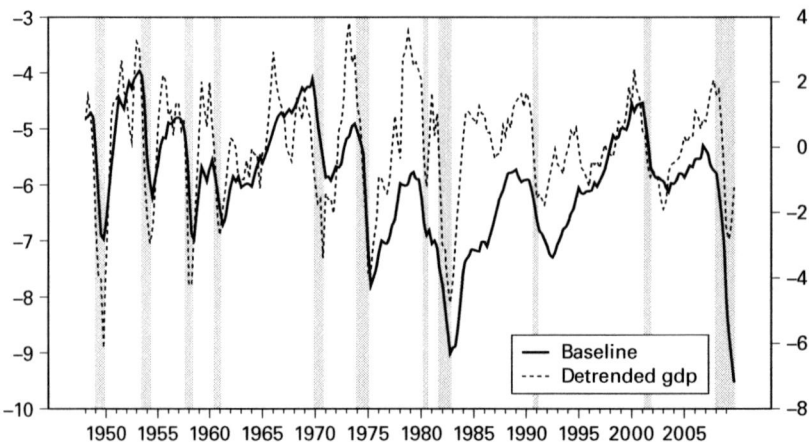

Figure 2.5
Output gap and detrended GDP: US evidence

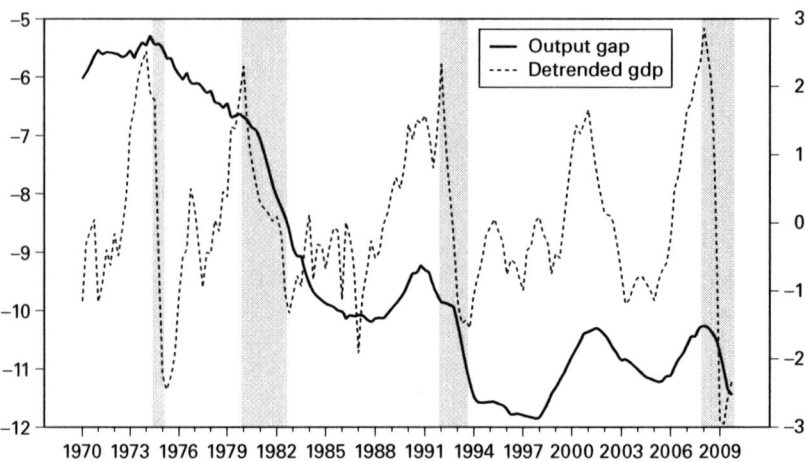

Figure 2.6
Output gap and detrended GDP: euro area evidence

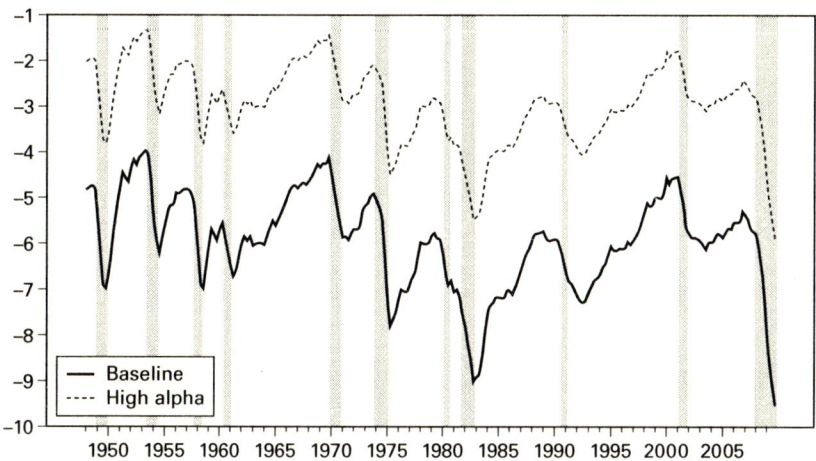

Figure 2.7
US output gap: Impact of α

model-based output gap.[6] The divergent paths of the two variables in the second half of 2009, with detrended GDP picking up while the output gap remains at an all time low, provide an illustration of that imperfect comovement between the two variables. As shown in Figure 2.6, however, the relationship between detrended GDP and the output gap breaks down for the euro area: the correlation between the two variables is only 0.13, with detrended output failing to capture the apparent nonstationarity in the output gap.

Figures 2.7 and 2.8 examine the sensitivity of the output gap measure to alternative settings α and φ. For the sake of concreteness, I restrict myself to US evidence. Figure 2.7 plots the time series for the US output gap for $\alpha = 0.25$ and

---

6. Note that detrended GDP measures have zero mean by construction and hence will leave the level of the output gap unidentified.

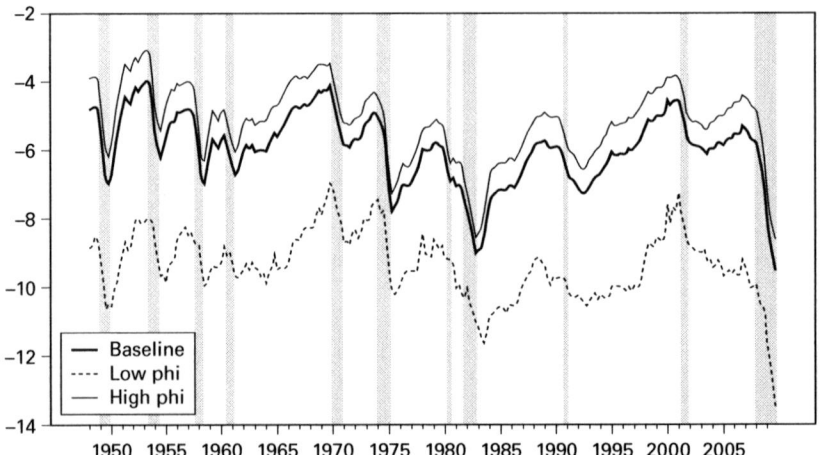

Figure 2.8
Alternative Frisch elasticities

$\alpha = 0.38$. The latter is the largest α value consistent with a nonnegative average price markup, given that the mean labor income share is 0.62. Thus, under the higher α setting, the *average* output gap is due exclusively to labor market distortions, which explains the significantly smaller output gap values (in absolute terms). However, the changes in the magnitude of the fluctuations, relative to the baseline, are hardly discernible.

Figure 2.8 plots the US output gap under three alternative calibrations of parameter φ, namely 1, 5 (the baseline setting), and 10. Those values arguably span the range of plausible settings for the Frisch elasticity $1/\varphi$. Parameter α is kept at its baseline value. A glance at figure 2.8 points to nonnegligible differences in the pattern of fluctuations across the three measures. Yet, as was the case in figure 2.7

the main difference relates to the mean of the series. In particular, a lower value for φ (i.e., a higher labor supply elasticity) implies a larger output distortion resulting from any given steady state price markup. That effect more than offsets the smaller output distortion associated with any given rate of unemployment, leading to a substantial increase in the absolute size of the output gap. The figure nevertheless makes clear that the output gap measure under $\varphi = 10$ is much closer to the baseline measure in both mean and patterns of fluctuations. Still, in all cases, the output gap displays a markedly procyclical pattern, reflected most clearly in the observed declines during recessions.

2.2 Unemployment, Fluctuations, and Welfare

In the New Keynesian model of chapter 1, variations in the output gap, as defined in the previous section, can only capture one component of the changes in welfare induced by deviations from the efficient allocation. A more complete account of the welfare implications of the latter should also take into consideration the implied variations in the disutility from work. This is what I set out to explore in the present section.

Let U_t^e denote the utility attained in period t under the efficient allocation. Next I derive an expression for the utility losses, $\mathcal{L}_t \equiv U_t^e - U_t$, generated by deviations from the efficient allocation due to distortions in goods and labor markets. Note that under the assumption of logarithmic utility on consumption, the utility losses thus defined can be interpreted as a compensating variation in consumption, expressed as a fraction of consumption itself.

Before I turn to the derivation of $\mathcal{L}_t$ it is useful to state the following Lemma.

Lemma 1 The following relationship holds:

$$\int_0^1 N_t(i)^{1+\varphi} di = N_t^{1+\varphi} \Delta_t^n,$$

where $\Delta_t^n \equiv \int_0^1 (N_t(i)/N_t)^{1+\varphi} di = \left(\int_0^1 W_t(i)^{-\epsilon_w(1+\varphi)} di\right) / \left(\int_0^1 W_t(i)^{-\epsilon_w} di\right)^{1+\varphi} \geq 1$, is a measure of employment dispersion across labor types.

Proof See appendix B.

The lemma implies that the household's overall disutility of labor is increasing in employment dispersion, in addition to the level of employment. This is a consequence of the convexity of disutility for each type of specialized labor service.

Letting $\delta_t^w \equiv \log \Delta_t^w$ and $\delta_t^p \equiv \log \Delta_t^p$, we can derive the following *exact* expression for the period utility loss:

$$\mathcal{L}_t \equiv U_t^e - U_t$$

$$= \log(Y_t^e/Y_t) - \left(\frac{\chi_t}{1+\varphi}\right)\left((N_t^e)^{1+\varphi} - \int_0^1 N_t(i)^{1+\varphi} di\right)$$

$$= \log(Y_t^e/Y_t) - \left(\frac{1-\alpha}{1+\varphi}\right)(1 - \Delta_t^n (N_t/N_t^e)^{1+\varphi})$$

$$= -x_t - \left(\frac{1-\alpha}{1+\varphi}\right)\left(1 - \Delta_t^n \Delta_t^{1+\varphi} \exp\left\{\left(\frac{1+\varphi}{1-\alpha}\right) x_t\right\}\right),$$

(2.12)

where the third equality makes use of the aggregate relation (1.20).

The first term in (2.12), which is minus the output gap, captures the utility forgone as a result of a lower level of output (and thus consumption) relative to the efficient allocation. That utility loss is partly offset by the lower overall disutility from work. This is captured by the second term

Unemployment, Output Gap, Welfare Costs of Fluctuations 53

in (2.12). In that term, Δ_t^n adjusts for the additional disutility caused by the inefficient dispersion of employment across labor types (which raises the overall disutility from a given level of employment), while Δ_t captures the additional employment required to produce a given level of output due to the inefficient allocation of resources across firms caused by the dispersion in prices and wages.

For the purposes of the present chapter, I will ignore the terms capturing the consequences of price and wage dispersion and will instead focus on the welfare effects of output gap variations. Thus, after setting $\Delta_t^n = \Delta_t = 1$, I can write the welfare losses as a function of the output gap, as follows:

$$\mathcal{L}(x_t) \simeq -x_t - \left(\frac{1-\alpha}{1+\varphi}\right)\left(1 - \exp\left\{\left(\frac{1+\varphi}{1-\alpha}\right)x_t\right\}\right) \quad (2.13)$$

Figure 2.9 plots the utility loss as function of the output gap, given $\alpha = 0.25$ and the three alternative calibrations for φ considered above (i.e., 1, 5, and 10). Though the utility losses are smaller than the output gap itself (due to the offsetting effect of a smaller disutility from work), those losses are far from negligible (recall they are expressed as a percent of consumption). They are also quite sensitive to the calibration of φ. In particular, a larger value of φ raises the utility loss associated with any negative output gap. Note also the convexity of the loss function, which penalizes output gap volatility. Figure 2.10 plots the same function against the unemployment rate, given a price markup fixed at its baseline steady state value (i.e., $\mu^p = 0.125$).

Notice in the figure that the sign of the effect of φ on utility losses is now ambiguous, and depends on the level of the unemployment rate. To understand that dependence, notice that an increase in φ (i.e., a more inelastic labor supply) lowers the utility losses resulting from goods market

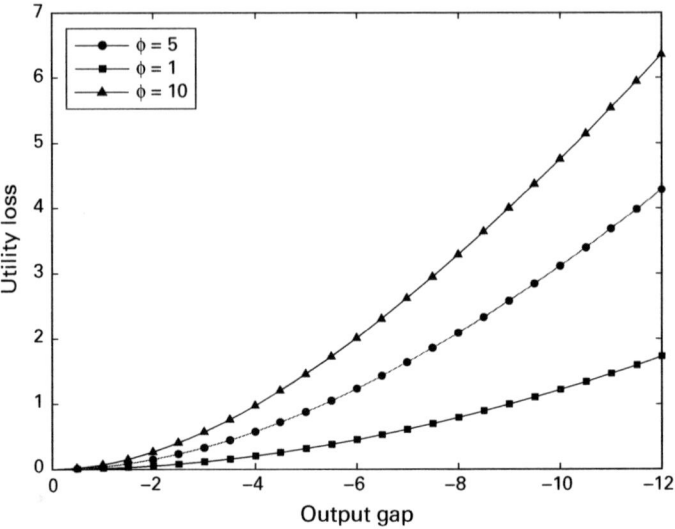

Figure 2.9
Utility losses and the output gap

distortions but raises the corresponding losses associated with unemployment. When unemployment is low, the first effect dominates. But when it is sufficiently high (above 4 percent, roughly, under the baseline calibration), an increase in φ raises the utility losses associated with any given unemployment rate.

Figures 2.11 and 2.12 display the utility loss generated by the observed fluctuations in the output gap in the United States and the euro area, respectively, based on (2.13) and for the three alternative values of φ considered above. The first row of table 2.1 reports the average utility loss in each case. Under the baseline setting for φ, the average utility loss for the United States represents 1.23 percent of consumption. As figure 2.11 makes clear, utility losses rise considerably during recessions, reaching a level above 2.5 percent

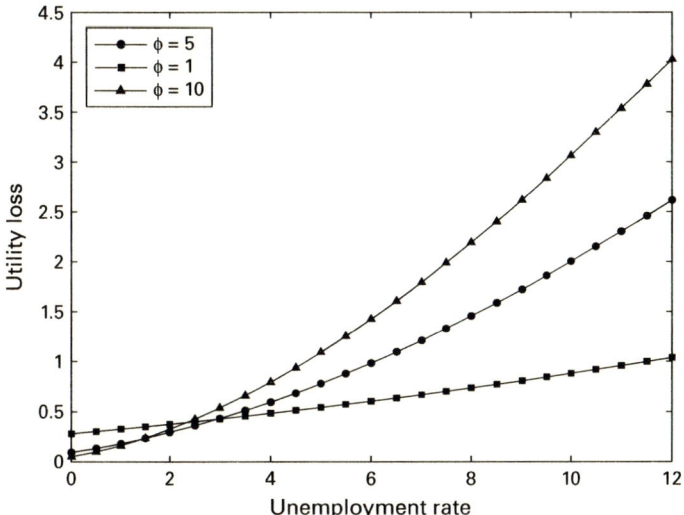

Figure 2.10
Utility losses and the unemployment rate

during the recession of the early 1980s as well as the recent recession. Notice that the corresponding average utility losses for the other two φ settings considered do not diverge much from the baseline, though their differences are more remarkable during recession episodes, as seen in the

Table 2.1
Output Gap Fluctuations and Welfare

	United States			Euro area		
	$\varphi = 5$	$\varphi = 10$	$\varphi = 1$	$\varphi = 5$	$\varphi = 10$	$\varphi = 1$
$E\{\mathcal{L}(x_t)\}$	1.24	1.58	1.08	2.76	3.08	3.19
$E\{\mathcal{L}(x_t)\} - \mathcal{L}(x)$	0.04	0.08	0.01	0.18	0.32	0.11
$E\{\mathcal{L}(x_t)\} - E\{\mathcal{L}(x_t \geq x)\}$	0.16	0.24	0.09	0.52	0.63	0.49
$E\{\mathcal{L}(x_t)\} - E\{\mathcal{L}(x_t + \Delta)\}$	0.22	0.34	0.08	0.31	0.43	0.13

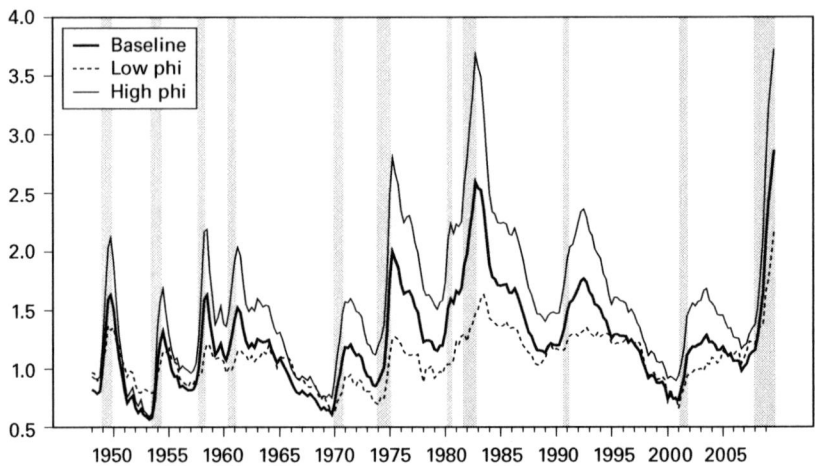

Figure 2.11
Utility losses and the US business cycle

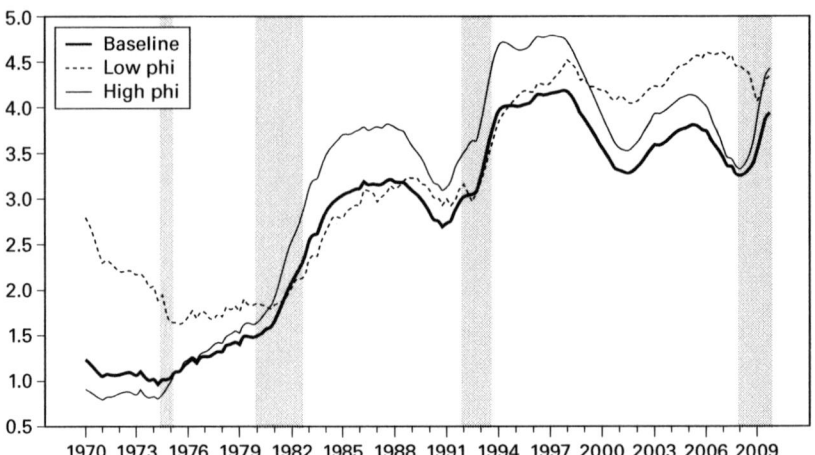

Figure 2.12
Utility losses and the euro area business cycle

figure. In the case of the euro area, the average utility loss under $\varphi = 5$ is 2.76 percent of consumption, more than twice as large as the United States. Figure 2.12 shows that utility losses in the euro area also tend to increase significantly during recessions, but—in contrast with the United States—they do not quickly revert back to their original levels in the aftermath. Of course, this mirrors to a large extent the seemingly nonstationary behavior of the unemployment rate in the euro area. Under the baseline calibration of φ the highest losses (of about 4 percent of consumption) are experienced in the mid-1990s, well after the 1992 to 1993 recession is over, and then again during the current recession.

Despite the nonnegligible average utility losses resulting from the distortions in goods and labor markets, and the significant variations in such losses associated with fluctuations, the gains in utility that would result from stabilizing the output gap at its *mean* value are very small. To a second-order approximation, the average utility loss per period resulting exclusively from the existence of fluctuations in the output gap is given by

$$E\{\mathcal{L}(x_t)\} - \mathcal{L}(x) \simeq \frac{1}{2}\left(\frac{1+\varphi}{1-\alpha}\right)\text{var}(x_t).$$

The second row of table 2.1 reports the values for such losses. Under the baseline calibration those losses amount to 0.04 percent of consumption per period in the case of the United States a very small value. The numbers are somewhat larger for the euro area but still of a similar order of magnitude: they amount to less than a third of 1 percent of consumption in all cases considered.

The third row of table 2.1 recomputes the average utility losses for a counterfactual output gap measure constructed by truncating the original output gap from below at its mean level, and compares them with the original average utility loss. The difference between the two represents the welfare gains from an asymmetric policy that would fully eliminate any negative deviations in the output gap from its steady state level, but leave unchanged the observed variations above that steady state. Not surprisingly, the average welfare gains from such a policy are a multiple of those generated from a policy that fully stabilizes the output gap at its steady state level, but they are still relatively small in absolute value, especially in the United States (though not so much in the euro area, where they are above one-half of a percentage point).

To provide some perspective on the magnitude of the welfare gains associated with such stabilization policies, the last row of table 2.1 reports the average gains in utility resulting from an increase in the mean output gap corresponding to a permanent reduction of one percentage point in the unemployment rate (e.g., as a result of a decline in the market power of unions). Such static gains are systematically larger than those that result from a complete stabilization of the output gap at its mean level.

The analysis in the present chapter illustrates some of the potential applications of the framework developed in chapter 1. In particular, we have seen how one can exploit the information contained in the unemployment rate to construct measures of the output gap and of the utility losses resulting from goods and labor market imperfections and their variations over time. There are several significant findings uncovered by that approach that are worth recalling here. First, the analysis points to large variations in the degree of efficiency of the economy, as measured by the output gap. In the United States that output gap is closely related to traditional measures of the business cycle, like

HP-detrended (log) GDP, thus confirming the findings in Galí, Gertler, and López-Salido (2007) and others. In the euro area, however, the output gap inherits the nonstationary behavior of the unemployment rate, thus displaying a much lower correlation with detrended (log) GDP and making the latter a poor proxy for variations in aggregate efficiency. The findings above also point to nonnegligible welfare losses from an inefficiently low level of activity, especially in recessions, and both in the United States and in the euro area. But the average costs of fluctuations in the output gap are small. This is so, in particular, relative to gains from a small permanent decrease in the unemployment rate.

3 Unemployment and Monetary Policy Design in the New Keynesian Model

In the present chapter I shift the focus to normative issues. In particular, I analyze the desirability of alternative monetary policy rules in the context of the New Keynesian model developed in chapter 1. To be clear, I am not the first to do so. Erceg, Henderson, and Levin (2000) have already derived the optimal monetary policy in a nearly identical model, and studied the welfare consequences of alternative (suboptimal) policies. Similar analyses can also be found in Woodford (2003) and Galí (2008), among others. That earlier work, however, did not make any reference to unemployment, since the latter variable was not even introduced explicitly in the model. The novelty of the analysis presented here lies precisely in its focus on unemployment. Two alternative perspectives are adopted in that regard. First, I analyze the implications of the *optimal* policy for the unemployment rate (in addition to other variables), in an economy buffeted by technology and labor supply shocks, and compare such implications with those obtained under a standard Taylor rule. Second, I study the performance of alternative *simple* interest rate rules, putting special emphasis on the potential gains from having the central bank respond systematically to variations in the unemployment rate, in addition to output and inflation. The latter exercise is motivated by two observations. On the one hand, several authors have shown that a policy that fully stabilizes the output gap constitutes a good approximation to the optimal policy in the EHL model, at least for plausible calibrations.[1] On the other hand, the analysis of the previous chapter has identified a strong link between the unemployment rate and the output gap. That connection could be exploited by the central bank by responding directly to variations in the unemployment rate, which is a directly observable variable (as opposed to the output gap).

3.1 A Loss Function for Stabilization Policies

I start by deriving a loss function for a monetary authority operating in the New Keynesian model economy of chapter 1. Following Rotemberg and Woodford (1999a) and Erceg, Henderson and Levin (2000), that loss function is based on a second order approximation to the utility of the representative household.

Recall the exact expression for the period utility loss caused by deviations from the efficient allocation, derived in the previous section:

$$\mathcal{L}_t \equiv U_t^e - U_t$$

$$= -x_t - \left(\frac{1-\alpha}{1+\varphi}\right)\left(1 - \Delta_t^n \Delta_t^{1+\varphi} \exp\left\{\left(\frac{1+\varphi}{1-\alpha}\right) x_t\right\}\right) \quad (3.1)$$

Next I derive a second order approximation to the previous expression around a zero inflation steady state with no growth. Note that in that steady state we must have

---

1. See, for example, Erceg, Henderson, and Levin (2000), Woodford (2003), and Galí (2008).

$\Delta^n = \Delta = 0$. For simplicity, and following Rotemberg and Woodford (1999a) and Erceg et al. (2000), among others, I also assume that such a steady state is characterized by an efficient level of activity; namely it satisfies $x = 0$. This can be guaranteed by a wage subsidy τ (financed through lump-sum taxes) that offsets exactly the distortions caused by market power in goods and labor markets. As shown in appendix C, this requires that condition $(1 - \tau)\mathcal{M} = 1$ is satisfied. It can be easily checked that under the assumptions made above, this condition also implies $x_t = \widetilde{y}_t$ for all t, for in that case the efficient and natural output coincide at all times. The reason is that once the distortion caused by market power is corrected, the only source of inefficiencies left is the presence of nominal rigidities.

The following lemma provides some auxiliary results that will be instrumental in deriving the second order approximation to (3.1), and in allowing me to write the central bank's loss function in terms of observable variables.

Lemma 2 Let $\delta_t^n \equiv \log \Delta_t^n$ and $\delta_t \equiv \delta_t^w + \delta_t^p = \log \Delta_t^w + \log \Delta_t^p$. Then up to a second-order approximation, in a neighborhood of the zero inflation steady state,

$$\delta_t^p \simeq \frac{\epsilon_p}{2(1-\alpha)\Theta} \, \text{var}_z\{p_t(z)\},$$

$$\delta_t^w \simeq \frac{\epsilon_w}{2} \, \text{var}_i\{w_t(i)\},$$

$$\delta_t^n \simeq \frac{\epsilon_w^2(1+\varphi)\varphi}{2} \, \text{var}_i\{w_t(i)\},$$

where $\text{var}_z\{p_t(z)\} \equiv \int_0^1 (p_t(z) - p_t)^2 dz$, $\text{var}_i\{w_t(i)\} \equiv \int_0^1 (w_t(i) - w_t)^2 di$, and $\Theta \equiv (1-\alpha)/(1-\alpha+\alpha\epsilon_p)$. In addition

$$\sum_{t=0}^{\infty} \beta^t \text{var}_z\{p_t(z)\} = \frac{\theta_p}{(1-\beta\theta_p)(1-\theta_p)} \sum_{t=0}^{\infty} \beta^t (\pi_t^p)^2,$$

$$\sum_{t=0}^{\infty} \beta^t \mathrm{var}_i\{w_t(i)\} = \frac{\theta_w}{(1-\beta\theta_w)(1-\theta_w)} \sum_{t=0}^{\infty} \beta^t (\pi_t^w)^2$$

Proof See Appendix D.

A first implication of the lemma above is that variations in Δ_t^n and Δ_t are already of second order, and a function of the cross-sectional dispersion in wages and prices. Taking the latter observation into account, we can write a second-order approximation to (3.1) around the zero inflation steady state as follows:

$$\mathcal{L}_t \simeq \left(\frac{1-\alpha}{1+\varphi}\right) \delta_t^n + (1-\alpha)\delta_t + \frac{1}{2}\left(\frac{1+\varphi}{1-\alpha}\right) x_t^2,$$

where, as in the lemma, $\delta_t^n \equiv \log \Delta_t^n$ and $\delta_t \equiv \delta_t^w + \delta_t^p = \log \Delta_t^w + \log \Delta_t^p$.

Furthermore we can write a second-order approximation to the representative household's welfare losses due to deviations from the efficient allocation as

$$\frac{1}{2} E_0 \sum_{t=0}^{\infty} \beta^t \left[\left(\frac{1+\varphi}{1-\alpha}\right) x_t^2 + \left(\frac{\epsilon_p}{\lambda_p}\right)(\pi_t^p)^2 \right.$$
$$\left. + \left(\frac{\epsilon_w(1-\alpha)}{\lambda_w}\right)(\pi_t^w)^2\right]. \quad (3.2)$$

Thus, as in Erceg, Henderson, and Levin (2000), the household's welfare losses are a function of the current and expected future values of the squares of the output gap, price inflation, and wage inflation. The first term measures the losses associated with the degree of inefficiency in the *level* of output, while the second and third terms capture the losses resulting from an inefficient allocation of labor effort across firms (due to price inflation) and across labor types (due to wage inflation). Furthermore the weights associated with price and wage inflation volatility are increasing (1) in the degree of stickiness of prices and wages (respectively), through their influence on λ_p and λ_w, and (2) in the degree of substitutability of goods and labor services (respectively), as measured by ϵ_p and ϵ_w.

As is well known, in the presence of rigidities in *both* prices and wages, the first-best allocation is generally not attainable, even under the assumed optimal subsidies. The reason is simple: an efficient allocation of resources across firms and labor types requires the absence of price and wage dispersion, which can only be attained if both wage and price inflation are zero at all times. But in that case the average real wage would have to be constant, which in the presence of real shocks will generally not support the efficient allocation. Determining the (second-best) equilibrium allocation under the optimal policy requires solving a dynamic optimization problem, task to which I turn next.

3.2 Optimal Monetary Policy

I characterize the optimal monetary policy in the economy described above, under the assumption of full commitment. The optimal policy is defined as the one that minimizes the central bank's loss function (3.2) subject to the constraints

$$\pi_t^p = \beta E_t\{\pi_{t+1}^p\} + \kappa_p x_t + \lambda_p \widetilde{\omega}_t, \tag{3.3}$$

$$\pi_t^w = \beta E_t\{\pi_{t+1}^w\} + \kappa_w x_t - \lambda_w \widetilde{\omega}_t, \tag{3.4}$$

and

$$\widetilde{\omega}_t = \widetilde{\omega}_{t-1} + \pi_t^w - \pi_t^p - \Delta \omega_t^n, \tag{3.5}$$

for $t = 0, 1, 2, \ldots$. Notice that the three previous constraints correspond to equations (1.22), (1.24), and (1.26), after setting $\tilde{y}_t = x_t$.

Let $\{\xi_{1,t}\}$, $\{\xi_{2,t}\}$, and $\{\xi_{3,t}\}$ denote the sequence of Lagrange multipliers associated with (3.3), (3.4), and (3.5), respectively. The optimality conditions for the optimal policy problem are easily shown to be given by

$$\left(\frac{1+\varphi}{1-\alpha}\right) x_t + \kappa_p \xi_{1,t} + \kappa_w \xi_{2,t} = 0, \tag{3.6}$$

$$\frac{\epsilon_p}{\lambda_p} \pi_t^p - \Delta \xi_{1,t} + \xi_{3,t} = 0, \tag{3.7}$$

$$\frac{\epsilon_w(1-\alpha)}{\lambda_w} \pi_t^w - \Delta \xi_{2,t} - \xi_{3,t} = 0, \tag{3.8}$$

$$\lambda_p \xi_{1,t} - \lambda_w \xi_{2,t} + \xi_{3,t} - \beta E_t\{\xi_{3,t+1}\} = 0, \tag{3.9}$$

for $t = 0, 1, 2, \ldots$ Those conditions, together with constraints (3.3) through (3.5), unemployment equation (1.25), the expression for the natural wage[2]

$$\omega_t^n = a_t + \left(\frac{\alpha}{1+\varphi}\right) \xi_t + \left(1 - \frac{\alpha}{1+\varphi}\right) \log(1-\alpha),$$

and the exogenous driving processes

$$a_t = \rho_a a_{t-1} + \varepsilon_t^a,$$

$$\xi_t = \rho_\xi \xi_{t-1} + \varepsilon_t^\xi,$$

characterize the solution to the optimal policy problem, given $\xi_{1,-1} = \xi_{2,-1} = 0$ and an initial condition for $\tilde{\omega}_{-1}$.

Figure 3.1 displays the responses of output, the unemployment rate, employment, the labor force, the average real

---

2. Note that in the natural equilibrium the (log) real wage will equate $\log(1-\alpha) + y_t^e - n_t^e$, which can be easily obtained using (2.6) and (2.7).

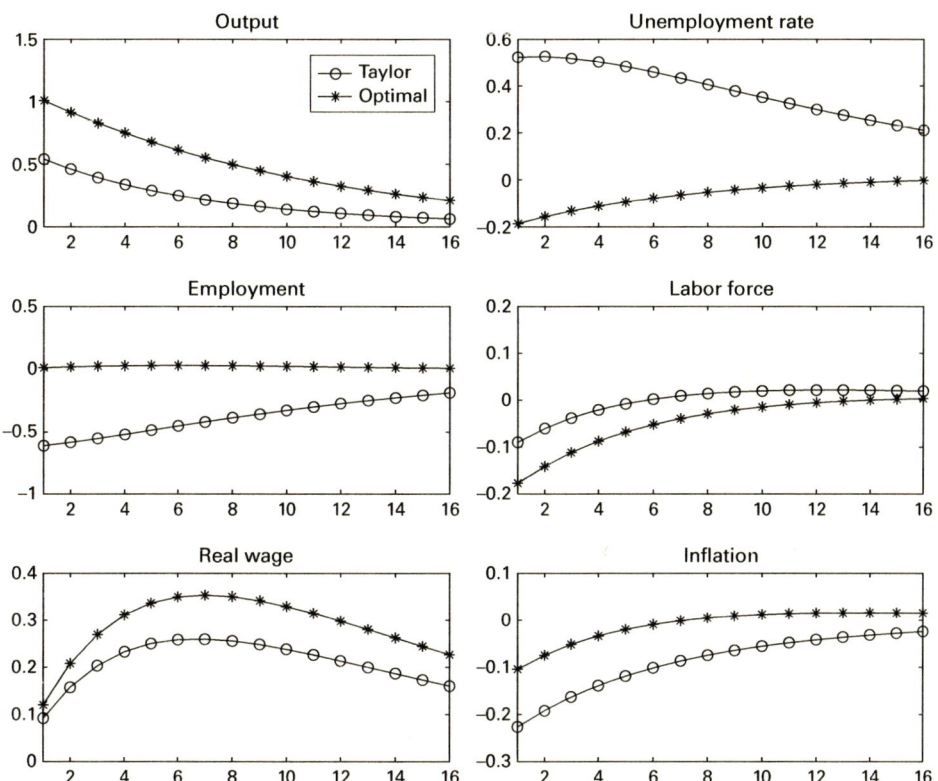

Figure 3.1
Dynamic responses to a technology shock: Optimal and Taylor compared

wage, and price inflation to a positive 1 percent technology shock, under the optimal policy, and given the baseline calibration introduced in chapter 2. For the sake of comparison, I also display the responses under the Taylor rule, shown earlier in figure 1.2. Note that the optimal policy is more accommodative of the productivity improvement than the Taylor rule, with output increasing more and employment

Table 3.1
Second Moments: Taylor Rule and Optimal Policy Composed

	Technology				Labor Supply			
	Taylor		Optimal		Taylor		Optimal	
	$\sigma(x)$	$\rho(x,y)$	$\sigma(x)$	$\rho(x,y)$	$\sigma(x)$	$\rho(x,y)$	$\sigma(x)$	$\rho(x,y)$
Output	0.66	1.0	1.30	1.0	0.23	1.0	0.79	1.0
Unemployment	0.75	0.96	0.23	−0.98	0.91	0.95	0.05	0.98
Employment	0.83	−0.98	0.04	0.68	0.31	0.99	1.06	1.00
Labor force	0.11	−0.92	0.21	−0.95	1.21	0.97	1.11	1.00
Real wage	0.31	0.53	0.42	0.62	0.16	−0.75	0.08	−0.60
Inflation	0.28	−0.99	0.12	−0.86	0.07	−0.99	0.03	0.87

remaining largely unchanged (as opposed to contracting) under the optimal policy. Notice also that the response of those variables is very close to the efficient one, which involves a zero response of employment and a one-for-one adjustment of output to the change in technology, as shown in (2.6) and (2.7). The figure also shows how the unemployment rate declines somewhat under the optimal policy, in contrast with the substantial rise observed under the Taylor rule. Due to the presence of rigidities in both prices and wages, the adjustment of the real wage is considerably muted relative to its natural counterpart (which moves one for one with technology), but is stronger than under the Taylor rule. This is caused by the larger upward adjustment of the nominal wage (facilitated by the lower unemployment rate) despite a more muted deflation (associated with higher activity, and hence higher marginal costs). The left panel of table 3.1 contrasts the statistical properties of some key variables implied by the optimal policy with those generated under the Taylor rule, conditional on technology shocks. Notice that both employment and unemployment (as well as inflation) are much less volatile under the optimal policy, even though output is more volatile as a result of the larger accommodation of the shock. Consistently with the impulse response functions shown earlier, we see that the correlations with output for employment and unemployment have opposite signs under the two alternative policies.

Figure 3.2 shows the response of the same variables to a labor supply shock under the optimal policy and the Taylor rule. As in figure 1.4, the shock corresponds to a 5 percent innovation in ξ_t, which would lead to a 1 percent decline in the labor force *conditional* on an unchanged real wage and consumption. While the labor force response is nearly identical under the two policies, we see that employment declines much more under the optimal policy, almost fully accommodating the response of the labor force and leaving the unemployment rate nearly unchanged. As a result wage inflation (not shown) is muted, leading to a weak response of the real wage. Price inflation remains practically unaffected by the shock under the optimal policy, displaying a slight negative response (which contributes to the real wage rise). Once again, the response of employment and output under the optimal policy can be shown to be very close quantitatively to the efficient response, as determined by (2.6) and (2.7), given by −0.83 percent and −0.62 percent on impact. However, and as in the case of technology shocks, the response of the real wage is more muted than its natural counterpart (the latter increases by 0.20 percent on impact, against 0.05 percent under the optimal policy). The previous patterns are also reflected in the right panel of table 3.1, which shows the relevant second moments under the two policies, conditional on labor supply shocks. In particular, the optimal policy implies a much smaller volatility

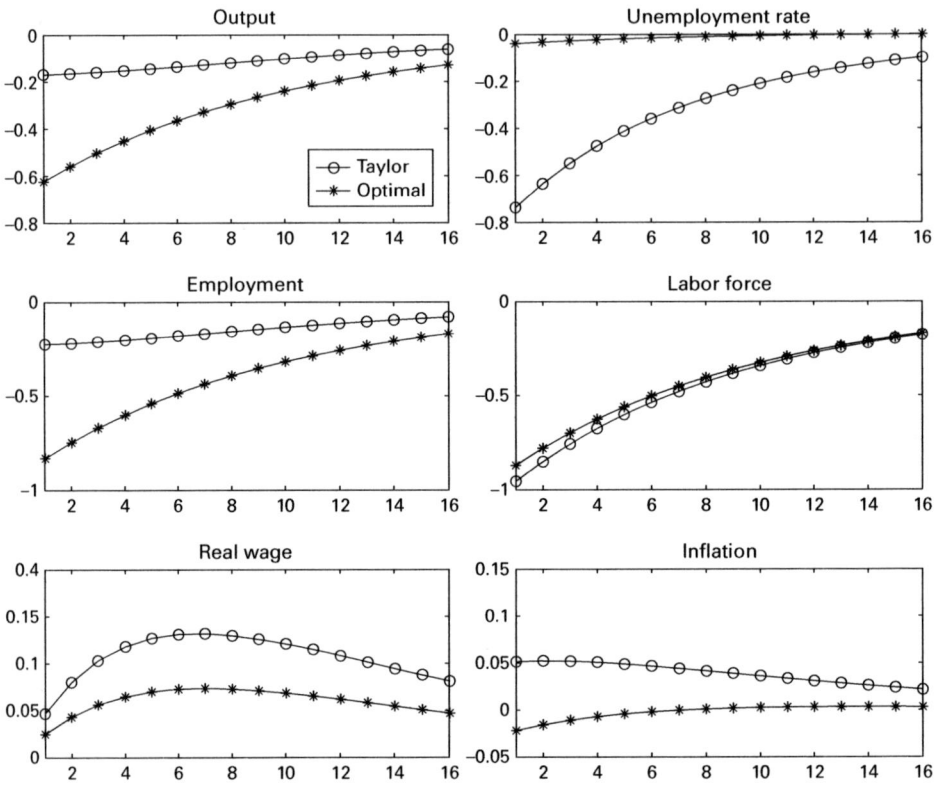

Figure 3.2
Dynamic responses to a labor supply shock: Optimal and Taylor compared

of unemployment despite the greater output volatility. That property is mirrored by the size of employment fluctuations, which are close to those of the labor force under the optimal policy but substantially smaller under the Taylor rule.

The previous analysis points to the desirability of a more stable unemployment rate than is implied by the conventional Taylor rule, in response to both technology and labor supply shocks. This observation motivates the exploration of the potential gains of introducing the unemployment rate as an additional argument in a simple interest rate rule.

3.3 Optimized Simple Rules

Following common practice, the baseline model developed in chapter 1 included a simple interest rate rule consistent, in specification and calibration, with the rule proposed by John Taylor, and widely known as the *Taylor rule* (e.g., Taylor 1993, 1999b). The Taylor rule is known to capture reasonably well the path of the federal funds rate in the United States during the early Greenspan period, though Taylor himself has pointed to substantial deviations of US monetary policy from that benchmark during the 2000s (more on this below). In the present section, I consider alternative specifications of the interest rate rule and analyze their properties through the lens of the New Keynesian model. Throughout, and in the spirit of Taylor, I restrict myself to *simple* interest rate rules, namely rules that describe the setting for the policy rate by means of a (parsimonious) function of observable variables. For each specification considered, and conditioning on each type of shock (technology and labor supply), I determine the settings of the coefficients that minimize the unconditional period utility loss given by

$$\left(\frac{1+\varphi}{1-\alpha}\right)\text{var}(x_t) + \left(\frac{\epsilon_p}{\lambda_p}\right)\text{var}(\pi_t^p) + \left(\frac{\epsilon_w(1-\alpha)}{\lambda_w}\right)\text{var}(\pi_t^w).$$

The interest rate rules considered are particular cases of the following general specification:

$$\widehat{i}_t = \phi_i \widehat{i}_{t-1} + (1-\phi_i)(\phi_\pi \pi_t^p + \phi_y \widehat{y}_t + \phi_u \widehat{u}_t + \phi_w \pi_t^w).$$

Table 3.2
Optimal Simple Rules

	Technology Shocks						Labor Supply Shocks					
	ϕ_i	ϕ_p	ϕ_y	ϕ_u	ϕ_w	Loss	ϕ_i	ϕ_p	ϕ_y	ϕ_u	ϕ_w	Loss
(1)		2.55	−0.06			4.15		3.22	−0.07			6.93
(2)	0.85	1.02	−0.06			1.31	0.60	1.11	−0.08			3.98
(3)		1.45	−0.13	−0.45		1.006		1.66	−0.08	−0.60		1.007
(4)	0.33	1.46	−0.12	−0.45		1.004	−0.22	1.33	−0.09	−0.31		1.006
(5)		1.46	−0.13	−0.46	−0.005	1.006		1.66	−0.08	−0.60	0.00	1.007
(6)	0.33	1.46	−0.12	−0.45	−0.01	1.004	−0.22	1.33	−0.09	−0.31	0.00	1.006
(7)		1.50		−0.50		1.106		1.50		−0.50		1.83

Table 3.2 reports the resulting optimized simple rules for a number of possible specifications of the latter. The implied utility loss, expressed as a ratio to the loss under the optimal policy, is also shown for each case. Row 1 in table 3.2 shows the optimized coefficients for a specification corresponding to the standard Taylor rule, with $\phi_i = \phi_u = \phi_w = 0$. Notice that under both technology or labor supply shocks, the inflation coefficient is positive and substantially above the one proposed by Taylor, whereas the output coefficient is small and negative. Welfare losses are between four and seven times larger than under the optimal policy.

When I allow for interest rate smoothing (row 2), the optimal value for ϕ_i is positive and high but still far from unity. The optimal inflation coefficient is above but close to one, while the output coefficient hardly changes. The implied welfare losses are reduced substantially but are still significantly above those generated by the optimal policy, especially when fluctuations are driven by labor supply shocks.

Row 3 shows the loss-minimizing coefficients when the central bank is allowed to respond to the unemployment rate. Notice that the optimal inflation coefficient is close to

1.5, the value proposed by Taylor, under either shock. The output coefficient is slightly more negative under this augmented specification but still relatively small. Most interesting, the coefficient on unemployment is negative and of nonnegligible size under either shock (−0.45 and −0.60, respectively). Furthermore the resulting rule involves only a tiny increase in the welfare loss relative to the optimal policy: the corresponding utility losses are only 0.6 and 0.7 percent above the optimal policy case). The previous finding is not significantly altered when I allow for interest rate smoothing (see row 4). It is also robust to allowing the central bank to respond to wage inflation, without or with interest rate smoothing (rows 5) and 6, respectively).

Figures 3.3 and 3.4 display the equilibrium responses of a number of macro variables to a technology and a labor supply shock, respectively, under the optimized simple rule shown in row 3 of table 3.2, namely that which responds to the unemployment rate, in addition to price inflation and output. For comparison purposes the responses under the fully optimal policy are also shown. Notice that the two sets of responses are nearly identical, suggesting that the optimized simple rule does a very good job at approximating the optimal policy.

The previous analysis points to the strong desirability of having the central bank respond systematically (and countercyclically) to the unemployment rate and inflation. However, the optimal response to output is very small, and with the sign opposite to the conventional Taylor rule. While the size of the optimized coefficients differs depending on the type of shock driving the economy's fluctuations, the differences are not quantitatively large, at least under the simple specification of row 3 in table 3.2. Motivated by this observation, I propose a simple interest rate rule with inflation and the unemployment rate as the only arguments, and

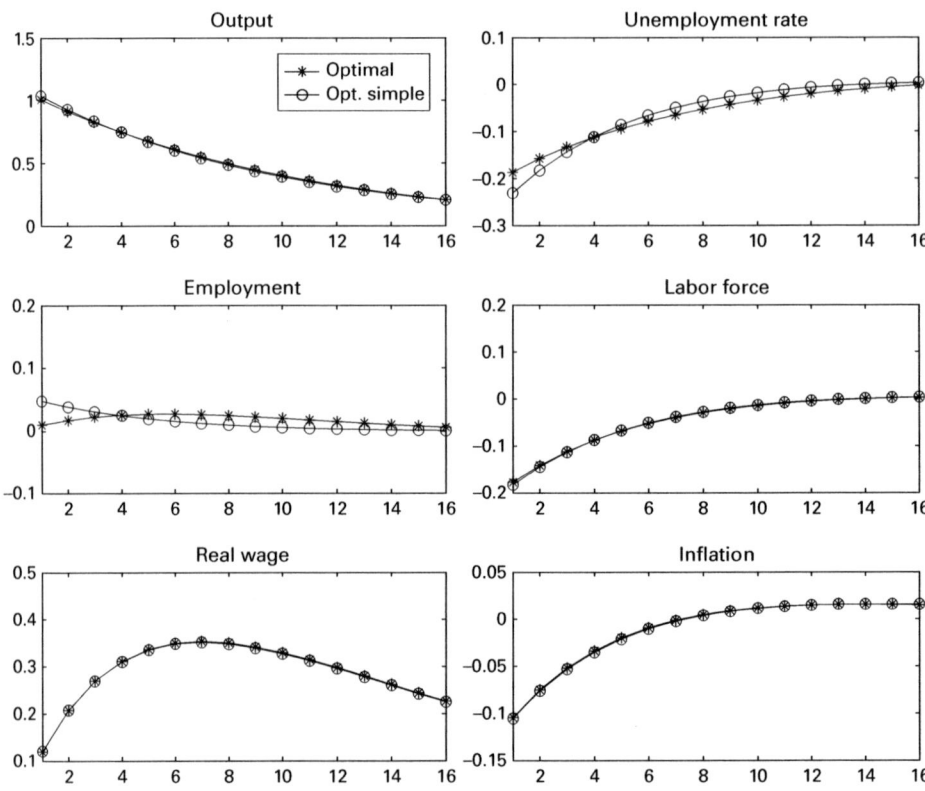

Figure 3.3
Dynamic responses to a technology shock: Optimal simple rule

with the associated coefficients lying somewhere between their values under the two conditional optimized rules. In particular, I consider the rule

$$\widehat{i}_t = 1.5\pi_t^p - 0.5\widehat{u}_t, \tag{3.10}$$

which I henceforth refer to as the "simple rule."

Unemployment and Monetary Policy Design

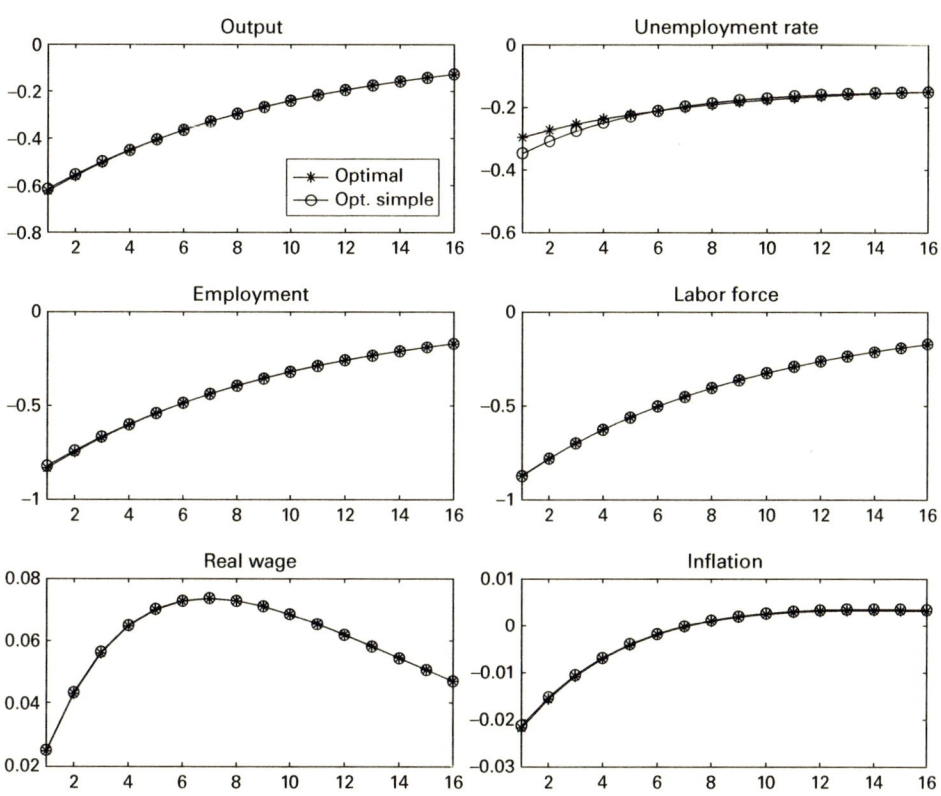

Figure 3.4
Dynamic responses to a lobor supply shock: Optimal simple rule

Not surprisingly, and as shown in row 7 of table 3.2, such a rule generates welfare losses that are somewhat higher than those implied by its optimal conditional counterparts (row 3). Yet the implied welfare losses are substantially smaller than under the optimized Taylor rules in row 1 of table 3.2, even though the latter are optimized conditional on each of the shocks separately. The good performance of

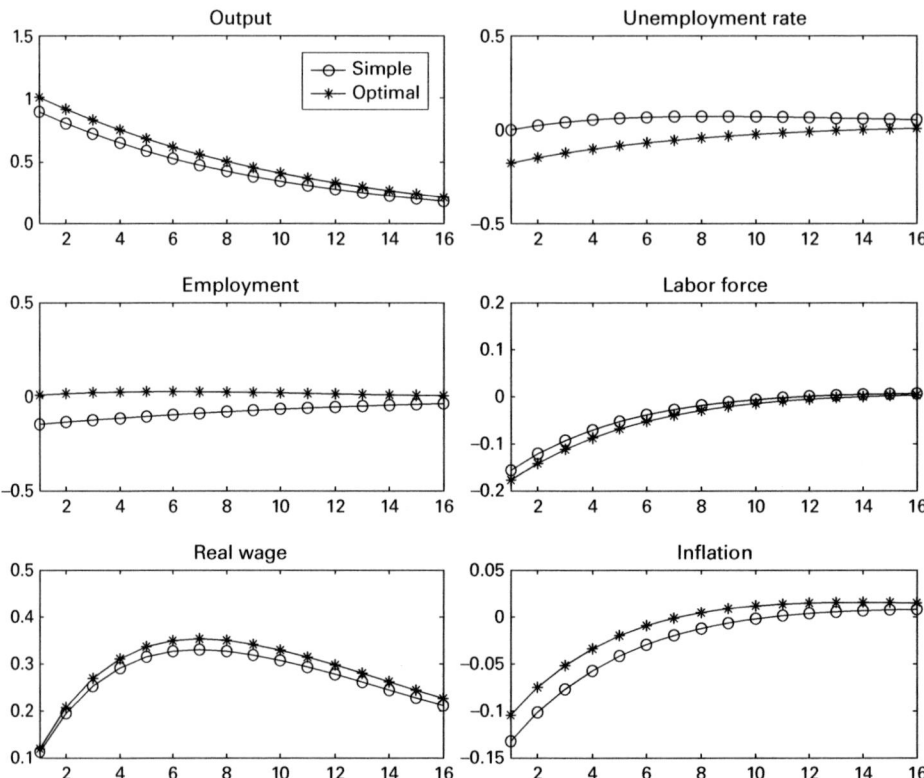

Figure 3.5
Dynamic responses to a technology shock: Simple rule

the "simple rule" is illustrated in figures 3.5 and 3.6, which compare the impulse responses to technology and labor supply shocks under that rule to those generated by the optimal rule. Though somewhat larger than those shown in figures 3.3 and 3.4, the gaps between the two sets of responses are quantitatively small, suggesting that (3.10) is indeed a "good" unconditional rule.

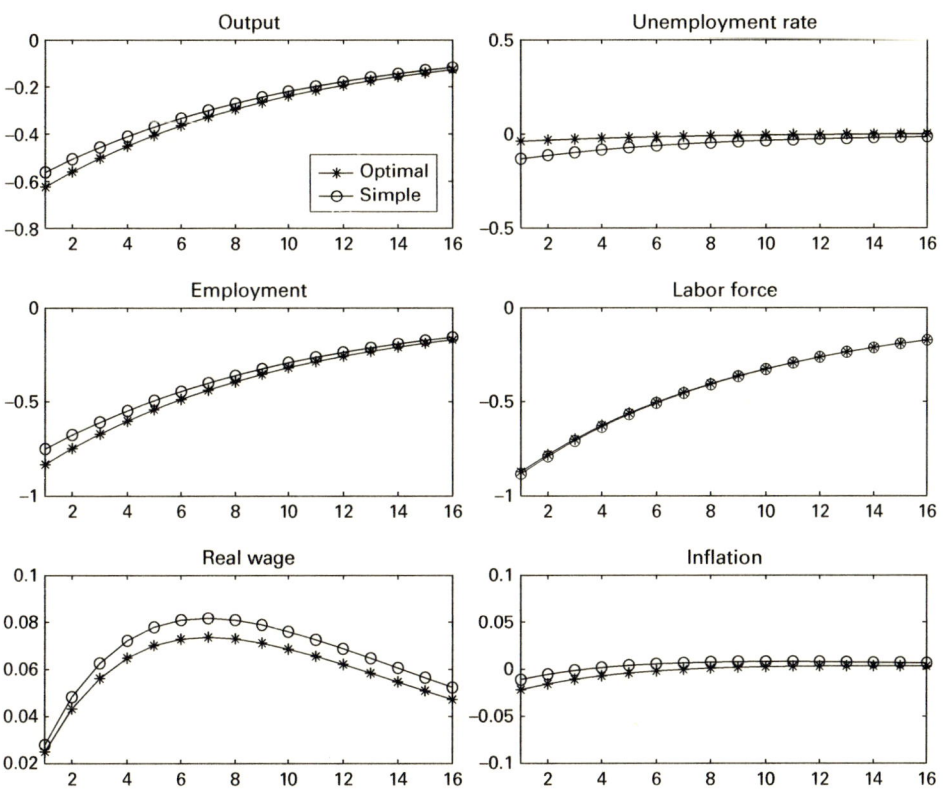

Figure 3.6
Dynamic responses to a labor supply shock: Simple rule

3.4 The Empirical Performance of the Simple Rule

I conclude this chapter by examining the extent to which the simple rule (3.10) can be viewed as a reasonable approximation to the interest rate policy of the US Federal Reserve during the Greenspan–Bernanke era or that of the ECB during its first decade of operation. With that purpose in mind,

I generalize the specification above to allow for a nonzero inflation target π^*. In addition I need to specify the steady state real rate, r, as well as an implicit target for the unemployment rate, u^*.

The proposed empirical rule takes the form

$$i_t = r + \pi^* + 1.5(\pi_t^p - \pi^*) - 2(u_t - u^*),$$

where i_t is now the policy rate (expressed as an annual rate) and π_t^p denotes *year-on-year* inflation, as in Taylor (1993). Notice that the use of annual rates for the interest rate and inflation requires that the unemployment rate coefficient be multiplied by four (relative to its value in (3.10)). As a measure of the policy rate, I use the federal funds rate target for the United States and the interest rate on the ECB main refinancing operations for the euro area. For both economies the GDP deflator is used to construct the measure of inflation, following Taylor (1993).[3]

After some informal exploration, I find that for the United States, a specification with $\pi^* = 1.5$, $r = 2$, $u^* = 6$ (from 1987Q3 to 1998Q4), and $u^* = 5$ (from 1999Q1 to 2009Q4) fits the path of the federal funds rate remarkably well, at least

---

3. Somewhat surprisingly, researchers have generally neglected the unemployment rate as an argument of interest rate rules, either in theoretical or empirical applications. A few exceptions are worth mentioning. Taking an empirical viewpoint, Fair (2001) estimates an interest rate rule that includes the unemployment rate in levels and first differences for the entire postwar period, and finds that variable to outperform traditional measures of the output gap. Rudebusch (2009) focuses on the crisis of 2007 to 2009. At a theoretical level, Orphanides and Williams (2002) analyze the properties of interest rate rules that respond to the unemployment gap (i.e., the distance to the natural unemployment rate), in levels and/or first differences, in an environment where the natural rate is unobserved. They motivate the use of unemployment instead of the output gap on the ground that the two are related by Okun's law.

until the early 2000s. This is illustrated in figure 3.7. Notice also that starting sometime around 2002 and until about the beginning of the financial crisis in 2007, the federal funds rate remained significantly below the rate implied by the simple rule, which might be suggestive of an excessively loose policy, consistently with the criticisms of Taylor (2009) and others. In contrast, for the period starting in 2008Q4—the quarter following the collapse of Lehman—the simple rule calls for an interest rate that goes well into negative territory, while the federal funds rate is constrained by the zero lower bound. This leads to an increasing gap between the two interest rates. Figure 3.8 compares the performance up to 2008Q4 (to avoid the distortion created by the zero lower bound) of the simple rule proposed above with the "standard" Taylor (1993) rule, given by

$$i_t = 4 + 1.5(\pi_t^p - 2) + 0.5\hat{y}_t,$$

where $\hat{y}_t$ is HP-detrended log GDP, as in Taylor (1999b). While it is clear from the figure that the Taylor rule also tracks reasonably well the broad movements in the federal funds rate, the fit is not as good as that of the simple rule. In particular, the mean squared deviation is 3.26 for the Taylor rule against 1.64 for the simple rule.[4]

Figure 3.9 displays the policy rate in the euro area over the period 1999Q1 to 2009Q4 to together with the interest rate implied by the simple rule above under the same

---

4. The mean absolute deviations are 0.95 and 1.56, respectively. Similar results obtain when I use a revised Taylor rule with a unit coefficient on detrended (log) GDP. The mean squared deviation for the latter specification is 3.11, while the mean absolute deviation is 1.46, both representing a tiny improvement over the baseline Taylor rule.

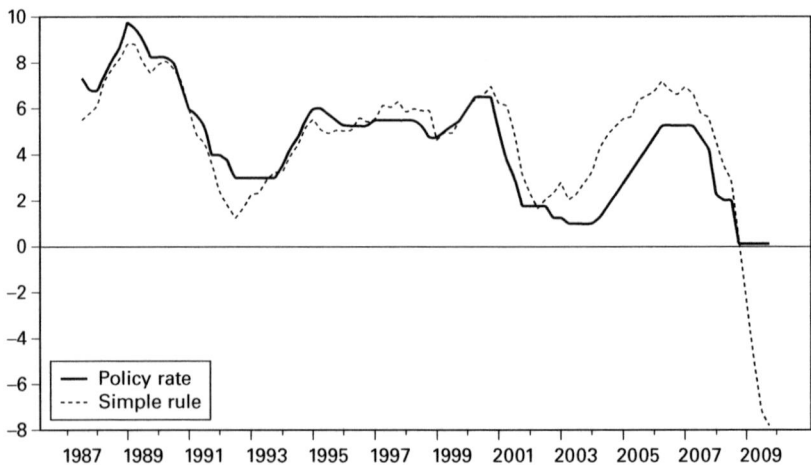

Figure 3.7
Monetary policy in the Greenspan–Bernanke era: 1987Q3 to 2009Q4

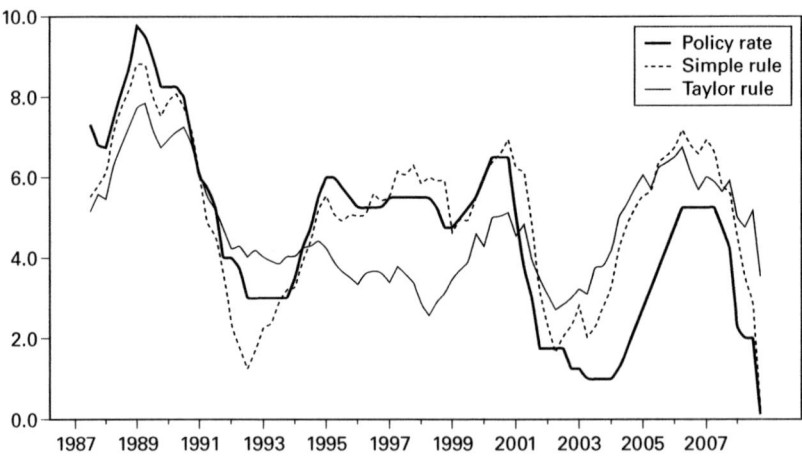

Figure 3.8
Monetary policy in the Greenspan–Bernanke era: 1987Q3 to 2008Q4

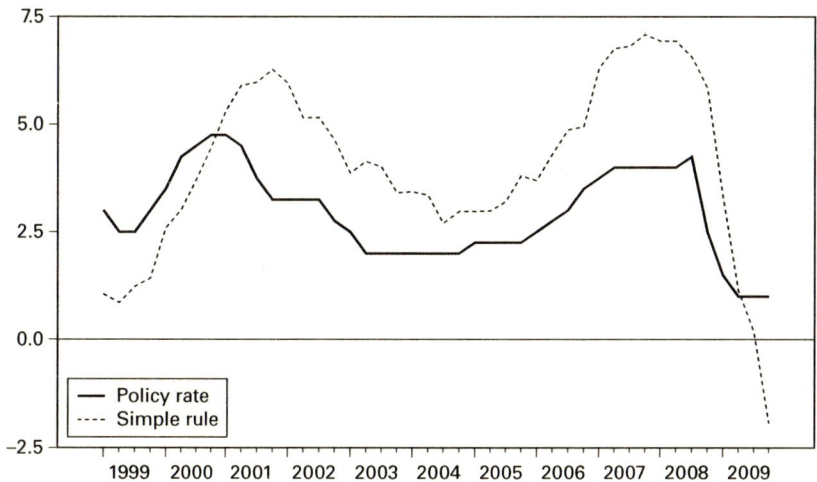

Figure 3.9
Monetary policy in the euro area: 1999Q1 to 2009Q4

assumptions for the steady state real rate and inflation target as in the US calibration ($\pi^* = 1.5$, $r = 2$), but with a target unemployment rate $u^* = 8.5$, which corresponds to the average unemployment rate over the period considered. While the fit is not nearly as good as it is for the United States, the simple rule manages to capture well the medium term variations in the policy rate and, in particular, the observed double-hump pattern. Taking the simple rule as a benchmark, the picture is suggestive of an excessively loose policy starting around 2001 and up until the start of the crisis. This observation is consistent with the contemporaneous analysis of some ECB-watchers (e.g., Galí et al. 2004). Notice further that the simple rule implies a negative interest rate after mid-2009, but one that is much smaller in absolute value than its US counterpart, suggesting that the zero lower bound has been somewhat less binding in the euro area.

Overall, the evidence presented above could be interpreted as suggesting that in conducting their policies, central banks (or at least the Fed and the ECB) have been paying more attention to the evolution of unemployment than most academic macroeconomists when designing their models.

4 Concluding Remarks and Directions for Future Research

In this book I have proposed an alternative approach for introducing unemployment in the New Keynesian framework. The proposed approach involves a *reinterpretation* of the labor market block of that model, as originally developed by Erceg, Henderson, and Levin (2000), as opposed to a significant modification of the latter.

Through a number of exercises I have shown how that approach can be used in practice to address many questions of interest. Let me next summarize the main findings in the form of bullet points.

• A calibrated version of the standard New Keynesian model has been shown to be capable of generating unemployment fluctuations that are "realistic" in terms of size and persistence. In the proposed framework those fluctuations are a consequence of nominal wage rigidities, since the latter prevent the average real wage from adjusting as much as it would be needed to keep unemployment constant at a the level consistent with desired wage markups. An empirically reasonable degree of nominal wage rigidities, corresponding to an average wage duration of one year, combined with the assumption of staggering à la Calvo and persistent shocks, are sufficient to deliver that result.

• Measures of the gap between output and its efficient level (i.e., the *output gap*) can be constructed using readily available data on the labor income share and the unemployment rate. The resulting empirical measures are positively (but not perfectly) correlated with HP-detrended (log) GDP in the United States but not so much in the euro area. Fluctuations in the average wage markup, mirrored in the unemployment rate, are the main factor behind output gap fluctuations at business cycle frequencies for both economies.

• While output gap fluctuations have been shown not to be too costly as such in terms of utility, the corresponding welfare losses associated with downturns are substantial.

• The optimal monetary policy in the context of the standard New Keynesian model with nominal wage and price stickiness implies a high degree of stabilization of the unemployment rate. This is true, in particular, when compared to a conventional Taylor rule.

• In the same model, a simple interest rate rule that responds systematically to both price inflation and the unemployment rate can approximate reasonably well the optimal policy.

While my goal in writing this book has been to defend a particular approach to the modeling of unemployment, I do not want to conclude that task without acknowledging some of its limitations, most of which—if not all—should already be clear to the sensible reader. Here are, in my view, the most important shortcomings of my proposed approach. The reader may also see them as pointers of directions for further research.

Concluding Remarks and Future Research

A first limitation of the model developed above pertains to its focus on a single source of unemployment, with regard to both its average level and its fluctuations: the presence of noncompetitive wages. In particular, labor market frictions of the kind emphasized by the search and matching literature are abstracted from entirely. The recent literature combining labor market frictions with nominal wage and price rigidities provides a natural starting point in order to overcome that shortcoming, but most of the existing models in that literature assume an inelastic labor participation, making fluctuations in unemployment the mirror image of those in employment. In other words, in the current models there is no information contained in measures of unemployment that is not revealed by observing employment. Introducing labor market frictions in a New Keynesian model with variable participation should thus be high on the agenda.[1] Estimates of that model could provide the basis for an empirical evaluation of the relative importance of frictions as opposed to wage rigidities as a source of unemployment fluctuations.[2]

Second, and as in the standard New Keynesian model, nominal wages in the model above are set unilaterally by workers (or the unions representing them) with no role given to bargaining. This is true in the original Erceg et al. (2000) model, as well as in all the extensions that have adopted their specification of the wage setting block.[3] That

---

1. Christiano, Trabandt, and Walentin (2010) and Galí (2011) are an exception in that regard.
2. See Michaillat (2009) for a first attempt at answering that question. His findings suggest that the frictional component of unemployment may be procyclical, with the rise of unemployment in recessions being entirely due to the sluggish adjustment of real wages.
3. That includes the "reference" models of Smets and Wouters (2003, 2007) and Christiano, Eichenbaum, and Evans (2005).

feature of the standard New Keynesian model seems to be at odds with the evidence on wage setting, both in the United States and Europe. Rather, extensions of the New Keynesian model that incorporate labor market frictions typically assume some sort of wage bargaining between firms and workers. Understanding the connection between wage markups, unemployment, and wage inflation in those frameworks, particularly in extensions that allow for variable participation seems an avenue worth exploring.

A third potential shortcoming relates to the model's implications for labor market participation. Thus, under the preferences introduced in chapter 2 and used throughout the book, the labor force (or participation), l_t, is implicitly given by the equation

$$w_t - p_t = c_t + \varphi l_t + \xi_t.$$

As pointed out by Christiano, Trabandt, and Walentin (2010), the previous specification is likely to be counterfactual; in particular, the evidence suggests that participation rises in response to an expansionary monetary policy shock while consumption rises more than the real wage (possibly due to the presence of price and wage rigidities). Galí (2011b) and Galí, Smets, and Wouters (2011) consider instead preferences related to those in Jaimovich and Rebelo (2009), which when embedded in a framework similar to that of chapter 2 give rise to a participation equation of the form

$$w_t - p_t = z_t + \varphi l_t + \xi_t,$$

where $z_t = \vartheta z_{t-1} + (1 - \vartheta) c_t$, and with parameter $\vartheta \in [0, 1]$ regulating the strength of the wealth effect on labor supply. For values of ϑ sufficiently high, the potentially counterfactual prediction of the baseline model above is overturned. Christiano et al. (2010) propose an alternative framework that incorporates unobservable search effort and incomplete consumption risk sharing, and that can be reconciled with the evidence of a procyclical labor force.

A final and possibly more important limitation of the framework proposed in this book has to do with the assumption of full consumption risk sharing. While widely adopted in the macro literature in order to preserve the convenience of a representative household, that assumption leads to the unpleasant prediction that in any given period unemployed individuals enjoy a higher utility than those who are employed, since the latter consume the same amount of goods but, in contrast with the former, experience a disutility from work. In the model I presented, this is nevertheless consistent with unemployment being "involuntary" under the maintained assumption that individuals care only about the utility of their household and act accordingly. But its convenience notwithstanding, both the assumptions of full risk sharing and extreme altruism within the household unit seem to be at odds with the evidence.[4] Developing extensions of the New Keynesian model that are consistent with the property that unemployed workers are worse off "as individuals" is thus an important challenge for future research.[5]

---

4. See, for example, Clark and Oswald (1994).
5. The framework proposed by Christiano, Trabandt, and Walentin (2010), where imperfect consumption insurance arises as a consequence of the unobservability of effort, is a good example of progress in that direction.

Appendix A

From the definition of the price index:

$$1 = \int_0^1 \left(\frac{P_t(z)}{P_t}\right)^{1-\epsilon_p} dz$$

$$= \int_0^1 \exp\{(1-\epsilon_p)(p_t(z) - p_t)\} dz$$

$$\simeq 1 + (1-\epsilon_p)\int_0^1 (p_t(z) - p_t) dz$$

$$+ \frac{(1-\epsilon_p)^2}{2}\int_0^1 (p_t(z) - p_t)^2 dz,$$

where the approximation results from a second-order Taylor expansion around the zero inflation steady state. Thus, and up to second order, we have

$$p_t \simeq E_z\{p_t(z)\} + \frac{(1-\epsilon_p)}{2}\int_0^1 (p_t(z) - p_t)^2 dz,$$

where $E_z\{p_t(z)\} \equiv \int_0^1 p_t(z) dz$ is the cross-sectional mean of (log) prices.

It follows that

$$\Delta_t^p \equiv \int_0^1 \left(\frac{P_t(z)}{P_t}\right)^{-\epsilon_p/(1-\alpha)} dz$$

$$= \int_0^1 \exp\left\{-\frac{\epsilon_p}{1-\alpha}(p_t(z) - p_t)\right\} dz$$

$$\simeq 1 - \frac{\epsilon_p}{1-\alpha} \int_0^1 (p_t(z) - p_t) dz$$

$$+ \frac{1}{2}\left(\frac{\epsilon_p}{1-\alpha}\right)^2 \int_0^1 (p_t(z) - p_t)^2 dz$$

$$\simeq 1 + \frac{1}{2}\frac{\epsilon_p(1-\epsilon_p)}{1-\alpha} \int_0^1 (p_t(z) - p_t)^2 di$$

$$+ \frac{1}{2}\left(\frac{\epsilon_p}{1-\alpha}\right)^2 \int_0^1 (p_t(z) - p_t)^2 dz$$

$$= 1 + \frac{1}{2}\left(\frac{\epsilon_p}{1-\alpha}\right) \frac{1}{\Theta} \int_0^1 (p_t(z) - p_t)^2 dz$$

$$\simeq 1 + \frac{1}{2}\left(\frac{\epsilon_p}{1-\alpha}\right) \frac{1}{\Theta} var_z\{p_t(z)\} > 1,$$

where $\Theta \equiv (1-\alpha)/(1-\alpha+\alpha\epsilon)$, and where the last equality follows from the observation that, up to second order,

$$\int_0^1 (p_t(z) - p_t)^2 di \simeq \int_0^1 (p_t(z) - E_z\{p_t(z)\})^2 dz$$

$$\equiv var_z\{p_t(z)\}.$$

An analogous proof can be used to derive the second-order approximation:

$$\Delta_t^w \equiv 1 + \frac{\epsilon_w}{2} var_z\{w_t(z)\}.$$

Appendix B

Proof of Lemma 1

Note that

$$\frac{N_t(i)}{N_t} = \frac{N_t(i)}{\int_0^1 N_t(h)dh}$$

$$= \frac{W_t(i)^{-\epsilon_w}}{\int_0^1 W_t(h)^{-\epsilon_w} dh},$$

where the second equality makes use the labor demand shedule implied by firms' cost minimization. Thus it follows that

$$\int_0^1 N_t(i)^{1+\varphi} di = N_t^{1+\varphi} \int_0^1 \left(\frac{N_t(i)}{N_t}\right)^{1+\varphi} di$$

$$= N_t^{1+\varphi} \frac{\int_0^1 W_t(i)^{-\epsilon_w(1+\varphi)} di}{\left(\int_0^1 W_t(i)^{-\epsilon_w} di\right)^{1+\varphi}}$$

$$= N_t^{1+\varphi} \Delta_t^n.$$

Appendix C

Derivation of the Optimal Subsidy

Letting τ denote the wage subsidy, the price markup will now be given by $\mathcal{M}_t^p = [(1-\alpha)(Y_t/N_t)]/[(1-\tau)(W_t/P_t)]$, which can be combined with equation (2.3) to yield the following expressions for employment and output:

$$N_t = \left(\frac{1-\alpha}{(1-\tau)\mathcal{M}_t \chi_t}\right)^{1/(1+\varphi)},$$

$$Y_t = \frac{A_t}{\Delta_t^{1-\alpha}}\left(\frac{1-\alpha}{(1-\tau)\mathcal{M}_t \chi_t}\right)^{(1-\alpha)/(1+\varphi)}.$$

Recall that under flexible prices and wages $\Delta_t = 0$ and $\mathcal{M}_t = \mathcal{M}$ for all t. Thus, under the assumption that $(1-\tau)\mathcal{M} = 1$, the natural level of employment and output correspond to their efficient counterparts, as shown in equations (2.6) and (2.7).

Appendix D

Proof of Lemma 2

Letting $\widehat{w}_t(i) \equiv w_t(i) - w_t$ we can write

$$\int_0^1 \left(\frac{W_t(i)}{W_t}\right)^{-\epsilon_w(1+\varphi)} di = \int_0^1 \exp\{-\epsilon_w(1+\varphi)\widehat{w}_t(i)\} di$$

$$\simeq 1 - \epsilon_w(1+\varphi) \int_0^1 \widehat{w}_t(i) di$$

$$+ \frac{\epsilon_w^2(1+\varphi)^2}{2} \int_0^1 \widehat{w}_t(i)^2 di$$

$$\simeq 1 + \frac{\epsilon_w(1+\varphi)(1+\epsilon_w\varphi)}{2} \int_0^1 \widehat{w}_t(i)^2 di,$$

where the third equality uses the fact that

$$\int_0^1 \widehat{w}_t(i) di \simeq \frac{\epsilon_w - 1}{2} \int_0^1 \widehat{w}_t(i)^2 di,$$

which follows from the definition of W_t.

$$\int_0^1 \left(\frac{W_t(i)}{W_t}\right)^{-\epsilon_w} di = \int_0^1 \exp\{-\epsilon_w \widehat{w}_t(i)\} di$$

$$\simeq 1 - \epsilon_w \int_0^1 \widehat{w}_t(i) di + \frac{\epsilon_w^2}{2} \int_0^1 \widehat{w}_t(i)^2 di$$

$$\simeq 1 + \frac{\epsilon_w}{2} \int_0^1 \widehat{w}_t(i)^2 di.$$

Thus

$$\delta_t^n \equiv \log \Delta_t^n$$

$$\simeq \frac{\epsilon_w(1+\varphi)(1+\epsilon_w\varphi)}{2} \int_0^1 \widehat{w}_t(i)^2 di - \frac{\epsilon_w(1+\varphi)}{2} \int_0^1 \widehat{w}_t(i)^2 di$$

$$= \frac{\epsilon_w^2(1+\varphi)\varphi}{2} \int_0^1 \widehat{w}_t(i)^2 di$$

A proof for the remaining results in the Lemma can be found in chapters 3 and 6 of Galí (2008).

References

Alexopoulos, Michelle. 2006. Shirking in a monetary business cycle model. *Canadian Journal of Economics* 39 (3): 689–718.

Barnichon, Régis. 2010. Productivity and unemployment over the business cycle. *Journal of Monetary Economics* 57 (8): 1013–25.

Basu, Susanto, John Fernald, and Miles Kimball. 2006. Are technology improvements contractionary? *American Economic Review* 96 (5): 1418–48.

Blanchard, Olivier J., and Danny Quah. 1989. The dynamic effects of aggregate demand and supply disturbances. *American Economic Review* 79 (4): 655–73.

Blanchard, Olivier J., and Jordi Galí. 2007. Real wage rigidities and the New Keynesian model. *Journal of Money, Credit, and Banking* 39 (1) (suppl.): 35–66.

Blanchard, Olivier J., and Jordi Galí. 2010. Labor markets and monetary policy: A New Keynesian model with unemployment. *American Economic Journal, Macroeconomics*, 2 (2): 1–33.

Calvo, Guillermo. 1983. Staggered prices in a utility maximizing framework. *Journal of Monetary Economics* 12: 383–98.

Casares, Miguel. 2010. Unemployment as excess supply of labor: Implications for wage and price inflation. *Journal of Monetary Economics* 57 (2): 233–43.

Chari, V. V., Patrick J. Kehoe, and Ellen R. McGrattan. 2007. Business cycle accounting. *Econometrica* 75 (3): 781–836.

Christiano, Lawrence J., Martin Eichenbaum, and Charles L. Evans. 2005. Nominal rigidities and the dynamic effects of a shock to monetary policy. *Journal of Political Economy* 113 (1): 1–45.

Christiano, Lawrence J., Mathias Trabandt, and Karl Walentin. 2010. Involuntary unemployment and the business cycle. Mimeo. Northwestern University.

Christoffel, Kai, and Tobias Linzert. 2005. The role of real wage rigidities and labor market frictions for unemployment and inflation dynamics. Discussion paper 556. European Central Bank.

Christoffel, Kai, Günter Coenen, and Anders Warne. 2008. The new areawide model of the euro area: A micro-founded open-economy model for forecasting and policy analysis. European Central Bank working paper 944. Brussels.

Clarida, Richard, Jordi Galí, and Mark Gertler. 1999. The science of monetary policy: A New Keynesian perspective. *Journal of Economic Literature* 37: 1661–1707.

Clark, Andrew E., and Andrew J. Oswald. 1994. Unhappiness and unemployment. *Economic Journal* 104: 648–59.

Edge, Rochelle M., Michael T. Kiley, and Jean-Philippe Laforte. 2007. Documentation of the Research and Statistics Division's estimated DSGE model of the U.S. economy: 2006 version. Finance and Economics Discussion Series 2007–53. Federal Reserve Board, Washington, DC.

Erceg, Christopher J., Luca Guerrieri, and Christopher Gust. 2006. SIGMA: A new open economy model for policy analysis. *International Journal of Central Banking* 2 (1): 1–50.

Erceg, Christopher J., Dale W. Henderson, and Andrew T. Levin. 2000. Optimal monetary policy with staggered wage and price contracts. *Journal of Monetary Economics* 46 (2): 281–314.

Fagan, Gabriel, Jérôme Henry and Ricardo Mestre. 2001. An area-wide model (AWM) for the euro area. European Central Bank working paper 42. Brussels.

Faia, Ester. 2008. Optimal monetary policy rules in a model with labor market frictions. *Journal of Economic Dynamics and Control* 32 (5): 1600–21.

References

Faia, Ester. 2009. Ramsey monetary policy with labor market frictions. *Journal of Monetary Economics* 56: 570–81.

Fair, Ray C. 2001. Actual Federal Reserve policy behavior and interest rate rules. *Economic Policy Review*, Federal Reserve Bank of New York (March): 61–72.

Francis, Neville, and Valerie Ramey. 2005. Is the technology-driven real business cycle hypothesis dead? Shocks and aggregate fluctuations revisited. *Journal of Monetary Economics* 52 (8): 1379–99.

Galí, Jordi. 1996. Unemployment in dynamic general equilibrium economies. *European Economic Review* 40: 839–45.

Galí, Jordi. 1999. Technology, employment, and the business cycle: Do technology shocks explain aggregate fluctuations? *American Economic Review* 89 (1): 249–71.

Galí, Jordi. 2003. New perspectives on monetary policy, inflation, and the business cycle. In M. Dewatripont, L. Hansen, and S. Turnovsky, eds., *Advances in Economics and Econometrics*, vol. 3. Cambridge: Cambridge University Press, 151–97.

Galí, Jordi. 2008. *Monetary Policy, Inflation and the Business Cycle: An Introduction to the New Keynesian Framework*. Princeton: Princeton University Press.

Galí, Jordi. 2011a. The return of the wage Phillips curve. *Journal of the European Economic Association*, forthcoming.

Galí, Jordi. 2011b. Monetary policy and unemployment. In B. Friedman and M. Woodford, eds., *Handbook of Monetary Economics*, vol. 3a. Amsterdam: Elsevier B.V., 487–546.

Galí, Jordi, and Mark Gertler. 1999. Inflation dynamics: A structural econometric analysis. *Journal of Monetary Economics* 44 (2): 195–222.

Galí, Jordi, Stefan Gerlach, Julio Rotemberg, Harald Uhlig, and Michael Woodford. 2004. *The Monetary Policy of the ECB Reconsidered*. MECB Series 5. London: Centre for Economic Policy Research.

Galí, Jordi, Mark Gertler, and David López-Salido. 2007. Markups, Gaps, and the Welfare Costs of Business Fluctuations. *Review of Economics and Statistics* 89 (1): 44–59.

Galí, Jordi, and Pau Rabanal. 2004. Technology shocks and aggregate fluctuations: How well does the RBC model fit postwar U.S. data? *NBER Macroeconomics Annual 2004*: 225–88.

Galí, Jordi, Frank Smets, and Raf Wouters. 2011. Unemployment in an estimated New Keynesia model. Manuscript prepared for the NBER Macroeconomics Annual conference.

Gertler, Mark, and Antonella Trigari. 2005. Unemployment fluctuations with staggered Nash wage bargaining. *Journal of Political Economy* 117 (1): 38–86.

Gertler, Mark, Antonella Trigari, and Luca Sala. 2008. An estimated monetary DSGE model with unemployment and staggered nominal wage bargaining. *Journal of Money, Credit and Banking* 40 (8): 1713–63.

Goodfriend, Marvin, and Robert G. King. 1997. The new neoclassical synthesis and the role of monetary policy. *NBER Macroeconomics Annual 1997*: 231–82.

Hall, Robert E. 1997. Macroeconomic fluctuations and the allocation of time. *Journal of Labor Economics* 15 (1): S223–S245.

Hall, Robert E. 2005. Employment fluctuations with equilibrium wage stickiness. *American Economic Review* 95 (1): 50–64.

Jaimovich, Nir, and Segio Rebelo. 2009. Can news about the future drive the business cycle? *American Economics Review* 99 (4): 1097–1118.

Justiniano, Alejandro, and Giorgio E. Primiceri. 2008. Potential and natural output. Unpublished manuscript.

Keynes, John M. 1936. *The General Theory of Employment, Interest and Money*. London: Macmillan.

King, Robert G., and Alexander L. Wolman. 1996. Inflation targeting in a St. Louis model of the 21st century. *Federal Reserve Bank of St. Louis Review* 78 (3).

Kydland, Finn E., and Edward C. Prescott. 1982. Time to build and aggregate fluctuations. *Econometrica* 50 (6): 1345–70.

Merz, Monika. 1995. Search in the labor market and the real business cycle. *Journal of Monetary Economics* 36: 269–300.

Mortensen, Dale T., and Christopher A. Pissarides. 1994. Job creation and job destruction in the theory of unemployment. *Review of Economic Studies* 61: 397–415.

Michaillat, Pascal. 2009. Do matching frictions explain unemployment? Not in bad times. UC Berkeley. Unpublished manuscript.

References

Mulligan, Casey B. 2002. A century of labor-leisure distortions. Working paper 8774. NBER, Cambridge, MA.

Nakamura, Emi, and Jón Steinsson. 2008. Five facts about prices: A reevaluation of menu cost models. *Quarterly Journal of Economics* 123 (4): 1415–64.

Orphanides, Athanasios, and John C. Williams. 2002. Monetary policy rules with unknown natural rates. *Brookings Papers on Economic Activity* 2002 (2): 63–118.

Phillips, A. W. 1958. The relation between unemployment and the rate of change of money wage rates in the United Kingdom, 1861–1957. *Economica* 25: 283–99.

Prescott, Edward C. 1986. Theory ahead of business cycle measurement. *Carnegie-Rochester Conference on Public Policy* 24: 11–44.

Rotemberg, Julio, and Michael Woodford. 1999a. Interest rate rules in an estimated sticky price model. In J. B. Taylor, ed., *Monetary Policy Rules*. Chicago: University of Chicago Press, 57–119.

Rotemberg, Julio, and Michael Woodford. 1999b. The cyclical behavior of prices and costs. In J. B. Taylor and M. Woodford, eds., *Handbook of Macroeconomics*. New York: Elsevier, 1051–1131.

Rudebusch, Glenn. 2009. The Fed's monetary policy response to the current crisis. *FRBSF Economic Letter*: 2009–17.

Sala, Luca, Ulf Söderström, and Antonella Trigari. 2010. Potential output, the output gap, and the labor wedge. Unpublished manuscript.

Sbordone, Argia. 2002. Prices and unit labor costs: Testing models of pricing behavior. *Journal of Monetary Economics* 45 (2): 265–92.

Shapiro, Matthew D., and Mark W. Watson. 1988. Sources of business cycle fluctuations. *NBER Macroeconomics Annual* 1988: 111–48.

Shimer, Robert. 2005. The cyclical behavior of equilibrium unemployment and vacancies. *American Economic Review* 95 (1): 25–49.

Shimer, Robert. 2010. *Labor Markets and Business Cycles*. Princeton: Princeton University Press.

Smets, Frank, and Rafael Wouters. 2003. An estimated dynamic stochastic general equilibrium model of the euro area. *Journal of the European Economic Association* (5): 1123–75.

Smets, Frank, and Rafael Wouters. 2007. Shocks and frictions in US business cycles: A Bayesian DSGE approach. *American Economic Review* 97 (3): 586–606.

Taylor, John B. 1993. Discretion versus policy rules in practice. *Carnegie-Rochester Series on Public Policy* 39: 195–214.

Taylor, John B. 1999a: Staggered price and wage setting in macroeconomics. In J. B. Taylor and M. Woodford, eds., *Handbook of Macroeconomics*, Elsevier, New York: 1341–97.

Taylor, John B. 1999b. An historical analysis of monetary policy rules. In J. B. Taylor, ed., *Monetary Policy Rules*. Chicago: University of Chicago Press, 319–41.

Taylor, John B. 2009. The financial crisis and the policy responses: An empirical analysis of what went wrong. Working paper 14631. NBER, Cambridge, MA.

Thomas, Carlos. 2008. Search and matching frictions and optimal monetary policy. *Journal of Monetary Economics* 55 (5): 936–56.

Trigari, Antonella. 2006. The role of search frictions and bargaining in inflation dynamics. Mimeo. Bocconi University.

Trigari, Antonella. 2009. Equilibrium unemployment, job flows, and inflation dynamics. *Journal of Money, Credit and Banking* 41 (1): 1–33.

Walsh, Carl. 2003. Labor market search and monetary shocks. In S. Altug, J. Chadha, and C. Nolan, eds., *Elements of Dynamic Macroeconomic Analysis*. Cambridge: Cambridge University Press, 451–86.

Walsh, Carl. 2005. Labor market search, sticky prices, and interest rate rules. *Review of Economic Dynamics* 8: 829–49.

Walsh, Carl. 2010. *Monetary Theory and Policy*. Cambridge: MIT Press.

Woodford, Michael. 2003. *Interest and Prices: Foundations of a Theory of Monetary Policy*. Princeton: Princeton University Press.

Yun, Tack. 1996. Nominal price rigidity, money supply endogeneity, and business cycles. *Journal of Monetary Economics* 37: 345–70.

Index

Aggregate wage index, 11
Average marginal rate of substitution, 12
Average nominal marginal cost, 19

Bernanke, B., 77
Blanchard, O., 36

Calibration, 24–25, 34, 50, 53
Calvo, G., 11, 84
Central Bank. *See* Monetary policy
CES. *See* Constant elasticity of substitution
Christiano, L. J., 86
Composite markup, 41–43
Consumption risk sharing, 9, 87
Constant elasticity of substitution, 8, 18

DSGE. *See* Dynamic stochastic general equilibrium
Dynamic optimization problem, 65
Dynamic stochastic general equilibrium, 7, 36

European Central Bank, 77, 82
  ECB watchers, 81
  main refinancing operations, 78

Efficiency gap, 39–40, 46
Efficient allocation, 51–52, 65
EHL model, 7
Employment. *See also* Unemployment rate
  aggregate, 21
  dispersion of, 52–53
  efficient level, 42, 63
Equilibrium conditions, 20–23
Erceg, C. J., 3-4, 7, 61–64, 83, 85
Euler equation, 10, 20
Euro area data, 31, 35, 39, 44, 57
Extensive margin, 7

Federal funds rate, 71, 78
Federal Reserve, 77, 82
Financial crisis, 79
First-order approximation, 14, 19, 21, 42
First-order autocorrelation, 34
Flow budget constraint, 10–11
Frictionless price markup. *See* Price markup, desired
Frictionless wage markup. *See* Wage markup, desired
Frisch elasticity of labor supply, 25–26, 50

Galí, J., 3, 7, 13–14, 17, 36, 38–39, 44, 59, 61, 81, 86
GDP deflator, 78
GDP, relative standard deviations and correlations, 31, 47–49
Gertler, M., 38–39, 44, 59
Greenspan, A., 71, 77

Hall, R. E., 36, 40
Henderson, D. W., 3–4, 7, 61-62, 64, 83
Hodrick–Prescott filter, 31, 47
Household's intertemporal optimality condition, 10

Impulse response, 24, 26, 32
  to labor supply shocks, 29, 75, 77
  to monetary policy shocks, 28
  to technology shocks, 27, 67, 74, 76
Index of nominal dispersion, 42
Inelastic labor participation, 85
Inflation. *See* Price inflation; Wage inflation
Inflation target, 78
Interest rate rule
  empirical performance of, 77–81
  including unemployment, 72–75
  optimized coefficients, 72–73
  simple rules, 71–72, 84
  Taylor type. *See* Taylor rule
Interest rate smoothing, 72–73

Jaimovich, N., 86

Keynes, J. M., 37
Kydland, F. E., 37

Labor
  aggregate force, 14
  demand schedule, 11, 18
  income share, 43–44, 50, 84
  union, 10, 18 (*see also* Wage setting)
Lehman, 79
Levin, A. T., 3–4, 7, 61–62, 64, 83
Log-linearization, 12, 19–20
Lpez-Salido, D., 39, 59
Loss function for a monetary authority, 62, 65

Merz, M., 8
Misallocation of resources, 39, 53
Monetary policy, 23
  alternative rules, 61
  endogenous response of, 29
  optimal policy, 61, 65–66, 68–69, 84
  under full commitment, 65
Monetary shocks, 26, 32–33, 34. *See also* Impulse response
Mortensen, D. T., 2

Natural level of output, 20, 23, 43, 63
Natural rate of interest, 21, 23
Natural rate of unemployment, 16, 36
Natural wage, 21, 23, 35, 66
New Keynesian model, 1, 38, 51, 71
  with evolution of unemployment, 8, 83
  with labor market frictions, 85, 86
  with staggered price and wage setting, 17, 39, 61
  with staggered wage setting, 13
New Keynesian wage Phillips curve, 17
Nominal interest rate, 20
  equilibrium dynamics, 23
Nominal wage rigidities, 11–12, 38, 63
  absence of, 16
Nominal wage, 10, 18

Index

Observed variations in total hours of work, 7
Output
  aggregate, 20–21, 42
  efficient level of, 38, 41–42, 63
Output gap, 20
  average, 50
  components of, 46–47
  equilibrium dynamics, 23
  fluctuation of, 44–51
  measuring the, 37, 39–41, 44, 51, 58, 84
  utility gains from stabilization, 57
  welfare relevant, 42–43
Output volatility under optimal monetary policy, 69

Participation rate, 14
Phillips, A. W., 17
Phillips curve, 17. *See also* New Keynesian wage Phillips curve
Pissarides, C. A., 2
Ponzi schemes, 10
Preference shifter, 40–42
Prescott, E. C., 37
Price Index for final goods, 10
Price inflation
  equation, 20, 22
  volatility and cyclicality, 31–32, 69
Price markup
  average, 20, 40–41, 43
  cyclicality of, 44
  desired, 19
  as function of the output and wage gaps, 22
  steady state, 51, 53
Price setting, 18, 19

Real business cycle theory, 37, 38
Real shocks, 23, 26, 68, 69
Real wage, 21, 83

response to technology shock, 27, 67
volatility and cyclicality, 31–32, 68–69
Rebelo, S., 86
Relevant stochastic discount factor, 19
Rotemberg, J., 44, 62–63

Sbordone, A., 44
Search and matching model, 26
Second-order approximation, 57, 62–64
Seperability of preferences, 9
Shapiro, M. D., 40
Shimer R., 36
Smets, F., 17, 36, 86
Solvency condition, 10
Stabilizing policies, 37
  welfare gains of, 57–58
Steady state, 12, 14, 19, 21, 62, 64
Stylized facts, 31

Taylor rule, 23, 26, 61, 67, 69–71, 79, 84
Taylor, J. B., 26, 71, 73, 78–79
Trabandt, M., 86

Unemployment fluctuations
  nominal wage rigidities and, 16, 24, 33–35, 83, 85
  optimal monetary policy and, 62, 69–70
Unemployment rate, 14
  autocorrelation and persistency, 35
  equilibrium dynamics, 23
  labor supply shocks and, 69
  output and wage gaps and, 22
  target, 78, 81
  technology shocks and, 26, 68
  volatility and cyclicality, 31–35, 68

Unemployment rate (*cont.*)
  wage inflation and (*see* New Keynesian wage Philips curve)
  wage markup and, 14–15, 41, 43
US data, 31, 35, 39, 44, 54
Utility loss, 51–53, 58, 71
  the business cycle and, 56, 84
  labor supply elasticity and, 53
  output gap and, 54
  of simple interest rate rules compared to optimal policy, 72–73

Wage gap, 21, 23
  equilibrium dynamics, 23

Wage inflation
  baseline equation, 13, 22
  equilibrium dynamics, 23
Wage markup
  average, 13–14, 25, 41, 43
  desired, 12, 16, 36, 83
Wage setting
  approximate rule of, 12
  first-order conditions, 11
Wage subsidy, 63
Walentin, K., 86
Watson, M., 40
Welfare implications, 39, 51, 59, 72
  output gap variations and, 53, 84
Woodford, M., 44, 61–63
Wouters, R., 17, 36, 86